THE SACRED 7

A Path To Finding The Wholeness Of Self-Identity

By
ANDREW WAYNE THOMAS ECKER

DEDICATION

The Sacred 7 is dedicated to the children and adult children of the War on Drugs, all the innocent lives that have been impacted by a culture of intolerance and incarceration. This book is dedicated to the millions of people with a family story of being Native American and no way to connect to their culture and the millions of people that have lost their lives to suicide and addiction.

Acknowledgements

My *Sacred 7*; Kathy, Dale, Elva, Evelyn, Leroy and Wayne thank you for all the teachings.

My fiancé, Monica, thank you for being my best friend and by my side through this entire process dealing with my misuse of English and helping to make the book happen. I love you.

My daughter, Bailee, you are the best of me and always a purpose in my life. I love you.

My aunts, Kathy, Patsy, Betty, Suzan, Diane thank you for helping me through some hard times.

My uncles, Wes, Frank, Don, David, Joe and Bobby each one of you taught me something in my life, thank you.

My Cousins, Frank, Amanda Anthony, Christina, Billy, Michelle, Dorrie, Mike, Denice, Joseph

The DRUM, thank you, for being my best teacher.

The LIPAN Apache Band and the tribal Elders Richard and Moises, thank you for keeping the stories alive.

The Community at Native American Connections, Patina Wellness Center, Uncle Ted, Leroy, Thomas, Dwight, Henderson, Carl, Glen, Glen Justy, Virgil, Benson. Thank you, for giving me a place to pray sing learn and speak my truth.

All the people that have supported me with encouragement, prayers and finances in bringing my story to life in the pages of this book. Thank you.

In love and gratitude.

Table of Contents

Dedication ii
Acknowledgements iii
Preface vi
Introduction vii

Chapter 1
Journey to Myself 1

Chapter 2
A Sacred Introduction 15

Chapter 3
Seeds of Destiny 25

Chapter 4
Awakening 49

Chapter 5
The Seven Sacred Containers 77

Chapter 6
Creating Your Own *Sacred 7* 109

Chapter 7
The Great Awakening 147

PREFACE

Before anything else, I want to acknowledge the lives of the people who have held onto the ancient traditions of identity that this book is based on. Without listening to the words of introduction spoken by my Native American relatives innumerable times in ceremony, the path of the *Seven Sacred Containers of Self-Identity*, or what I now call *The Sacred 7* would still be dark to me and the questions that led to an infinite number of hours in prayer and meditation that have gone into this book would still lie dormant in the darkness of unlived potential. It is through the resilient lives of these unstoppable people that *The Sacred* originated. Through them, I was able to find my way to remembering the power of what it means to know myself and to birth this book. For that, I am forever humbled and grateful.

It is amazing to me to think about the struggle of this teaching and what it has gone through to get where it is now. My ancestral connection to these tribal ways goes back to the land now called Texas and to the *Apache Nde* people of those ancestral lands. They were the first of all the *Apache* people to have contact with the United States settlers, suffering the hardship of brutal war, yet they kept our tribal heritage and connection alive. I am so grateful for the stories from my family and for those who remained strong in defiance of the ravages of cultural eradication and genocide.

INTRODUCTION

Many of us go through a confusing and painful process of trying to find ourselves. Swayed by the influences of our culture's environmental, social, and spiritual pollution, we have been left drunk on pain, immersed in victimhood, and captive to suffering. With all that this modern age has to offer, so many of us have lost connection and relationship to the things that matter most. *The Sacred 7* offers a foundation and a path for opening our hearts and freeing our spirits and for building relationships with what is most sacred and true in life. It can provide a means to profoundly connect with the people in our lives, the world we walk through every day, and our innermost true self.

One way or another, I have been working with the ancient tribal technology of *The Sacred 7* for my entire life. It began the first time I asked *Who am I?* And *What am I?* The journey of *The Sacred 7* is one that begins with these profound questions. It has taken me into many experiences of self-realization, and its spiritual power has pushed me, provoked me, and even dragged me into a journey that has brought me a deep sense of self-awareness that continues to evolve to this day

This sacred technology honors everyone as a human being within a common family and with a genetic connection to the land. It is a process that calls from deep within us to unravel what is not true of us, to free us from that which we are captive, and to weave a new identity that gives us meaning, connection, and wisdom. Once you align with its power and purpose, it becomes a part of the fabric of your own human development and growth.

I have discovered myself through this sacred path. In the process, I've let go of much of the burden and confusion that are born of the illusion of self-identity and been able to embrace more of my truest self than I ever thought possible. By learning this ancestral tool, I have expanded and walked away from what was imprisoning me physically, emotionally, and spiritually. It has allowed me to create a fluid interaction with energy and has opened me up to the vast presence of higher guidance and wisdom.

Through my years of experience with *The Seven Sacred Containers of Self-Identity*, I have been able to embrace the medicine of my childhood abuse and neglect and find a profound comfort to ease my heart and fortify my spirit. *The Sacred 7* has been my staff and my partner. It carried me when the pain of religion and its bureaucracy had left me spiritually drained and empty. It has been the voice of encouragement when the illusion of self-isolation yelled within my mind, *NO ONE UNDERSTANDS YOU!* It has guided me forward when the counselors, ministers, and good people of my life have had no words of wisdom worth listening to.

I've learned that the experiences of life are not out to destroy us; that is not the plan of a loving and benevolent *Creator*. We go through our hardships to bring us strength and perseverance and to draw us closer to one another and to the *Source* that has infinite love for all. The more I understand the endless possibilities that lay within our minds, the more I understand how critically important the concepts within this ancient tribal form of introduction are to our current, contemporary lives.

The Seven Sacred Containers of Self-Identity is a powerful transformational tool that recognizes that you and you alone are responsible for molding and creating the energetic manifestation of who you are to serve your optimal design. It moves you out of the victim mentality into a consciousness of wholeness, relationship, and flow. The process has taught me to embrace my victimhood. It gave me the tools to transform the energy that, for years, was so dense that it felt literally like a black hole into a vulnerability that laid open my heart so it could be loved, nurtured, and healed. It became a natural and authentic process to transmute the energy of many of my past traumas.

In the practice of *The Sacred 7*, we intentionally call in and build an understanding of ourselves that draws from the wisdom and expansiveness of the seven directions as well as from the medicine of our personal lineage. We build an identity formulated upon the truths and the highest possibility of each of the aspects of self, which puts us in a place of powerful vulnerability, creation, and relationship. This perspective equips us with an ability to stand in our boldness and find our faith in our life process. It did for me, and I believe it will for you, too.

When the power and purpose of *The Sacred 7 are unleashed* within you, you are enriched by your past instead of being a victim of it, depressed by it, or reactive and triggered by it. It opens you up to experiencing a new depth in relationships to everything around you—from the smallest of the elements to the bigger than life people around you, from the rays of the sunshine to the kiss of the wind. Within the thread of ancestral connection of *The Sacred 7*, you discover your most empowered self.

Like the *Way of Beauty*, an ancient practice of my *Nde*

(Apache) ancestors, *the Sacred 7* is a journey of finding the beauty within yourself and your relationships. With practice and intention, you create a foundation that expands your consciousness and frees you from limiting and painful misconceptions and patterns. You allow the beauty and perfection of the archetypes of the seven directions to flow through you powerfully and naturally, so you can embody your highest self.

In the many years of service to community that this life has allowed me to have, I have been able to help countless individuals align with and discover the power of *The Sacred 7*. Now, I want to share this meaningful practice in the hopes that you will become empowered to share it as well.

It is my hope that in your exploration of *The Seven Sacred Containers* that your life will begin to flow like water and that the medicine of your soul blossoms for you and those you touch. My guess is that you have learned a lot already from the teachings within your life path and from the guides that have helped you along the way. Yet, if you're like me, you too hunger for more God experience. I believe that you will find that these *Seven Sacred Containers* give you the structure, connection, and medicine that is uniquely yours to do just that.

This book is for those who are called to go deep within their own spiritual development to unleash a sense of freedom and empowerment beyond what is offered in our everyday culture. Within its pages, I share with you a unique path that is both ancient in origin yet applicable to a contemporary lifestyle. It can help you open to a transcendental state of consciousness and an understanding of who you really are. As you read this book, you will be creating the fullness of the *I AM* presence within you, as well as broadening your vision of yourself and what it means to be a being connected to the physical roots of your being.

Now is the time for each of us to go boldly into the heart of our collective field of experience and find the medicine within ourselves to heal our world. It is time to find the beauty through the spears of hatred and trauma, and the arrows of betrayal. It is time to use technologies such as *The Sacred 7* to dive deep within the body of emotion we carry and process the dense energies that bind us in the captivity of the soul.

Go boldly with me now and discover the power and beauty you hold within!

CHAPTER 1

JOURNEY TO MYSELF

Smoke from the fire in the *Hogan* burned my eyes and filled my nostrils. Philmore Bluehouse, a *Navajo* elder and our host for the evening, said something in *Navajo* that I didn't understand to the young man who was building the fire. The young man reached for a broom and began to sweep the dirt floor. For a while, I watched him move his broom with intention and delicate movements. As a mixture of smoke and dirt filled the air, I breathed it into my lungs, and it felt somehow familiar. I felt comforted.

I had arrived early to ensure myself a good spot. Our host had personally invited about 150 people to his ancestral *Hogan* for a ceremony. The round dwelling was constructed of wood and clay and consisted of a single room, about 30' x 30' in size. The floors were simply the natural earth and the space could comfortably accommodate a small family. Of the 150 people who had been invited to the gathering, only about 30 were in attendance. We crowded into the small space, and I felt grateful that I had secured a place for myself early.

As I looked around the circle, I saw a rainbow of faces. There were a few elders from the community who had come to sit with us, but the rest were a mixed group of travelers and spiritual seekers. They looked as if they were awaiting the words of a sage. Some had been drawn to the mystic nature of our circle and some were there seeking healing.

Many of those in attendance had travelled from all over the world, some all the way from Europe and some from Australia, specifically to participate in the Gathering of Healers that would be taking place nearby in the Four Corners region of Northern Arizona, near Window Rock, the beautiful capital city of the sovereign *Navajo Nation*. They came from a wide range of professional backgrounds. Like me, they were drawn to experience the ancient ways and wisdom of the *Dineh (Navajo)* people directly. They came to learn from the *Dineh* healers, and others like myself, who were using the workings of energy and spirit to help transform individuals, families, communities, and the planet.

I had been invited to the Gathering of Healers for my drumming. I would be among many healers and medicine people of all kinds—from neo-shaman people of European descent to those whose grandparents had taught them traditional healing practices handed down for thousands of years. It was a unique calling of many different energies that were all brought together for a common purpose: to learn from one another and to make the world a little a better in our own unique way.

The drum has been a teacher, a friend, and a constant in my life for many years, so it was only fitting that the drum would be the reason that I started my deep journey in this ancient land. Drumming is my life's work and passion, and it may be the reason I am alive. I have been trained in several styles of drumming, including Native American, West African, Middle Eastern, and Latin. I've received training in drum circle facilitation from *Village Music Circles* and *Health Rhythms*, the first evidenced-based healing modality that uses recreational music. By the time of the Gathering of the Healers, I was already an accomplished facilitator with well over 2000 professional facilitations under my belt. Most of my work has been with the sick and institutionalized—those in hospital settings, memory care facilities, psychiatric lockdowns, cancer facilities, skilled nursing, end of life care, and the occasional prison and school. My many mentors helped me to relate this ancient practice to the modern language of the institutions. Their ways legitimized for the contemporary culture the ancient tribal technologies and have led to countless lives being changed and the world becoming a much better place. By learning the science of drumming, I was able to enter these institutions and bring the magic to the people that needed it. By 2012, I was facilitating one to five drum circles a day in Phoenix, Arizona and loving my life.

So, I had filled my van with drums and other instruments and took off to the Gathering of Healers. I travelled with my friend and fellow drum circle facilitator, Lynn. As we grew closer to the destination, a gracious sign appeared on the side of the road. *Welcome to Navajo Nation*, it said. I pulled my van off the road, got out, and laid down a tobacco offering to the land, in gratitude for our safe travels. I felt connected to the lands in a mysterious way.

We traveled several hours that day to reach our destination in the Navajo Reservation, outside Fort Defiance, Arizona, near Window Rock. The drive from the bustling city of Phoenix to the seemingly ancient and timeless lands of the *Dineh* people might as well have taken hundreds of years. As we got closer, the terrain grew more spectacular. The landscapes were painted with stunning red rocks and ancient volcanoes. It was truly a sight to behold.

Window Rock Monument is named for its impressive and mesmerizing natural structure made of red rock. The mysterious opening in the hard rock stands like a window into a higher level of self-understanding, mastery, and clarity. When I stood before it, it seemed as a sign, reminding me that a powerful mystery was unfolding in the energetic and spiritual workings of my life. The monument stood like a spiritual portal; I could feel it helping me to fortify my internal conscious voice—the voice that leads the pilgrim and guides the traveler.

At the same time, I felt a strange conflict arise from within deep within me. While I was surrounded by the utmost beauty and magnificence of the land, I could also feel the pain that had been endured there. I felt the trauma, and I felt the remnants of terrible bloodshed of the gentle people who lived upon it. I felt a deep sadness for the place. It was a place where the evidence of God was everywhere; yet it was a place that was invaded and taken from the people who loved and lived it.

The people who made their home there were bound up in these places—these *reservations*, as others called them—instead of enjoying the freedom to roam free, as was their way. I kept asking myself, *How could this happen to such a place, to such beautiful people? How could I see beauty here where so much had been lost?* I felt a tremendous connection to my Native American heritage in those moments. And I felt an outrage for my people and for our land.

My feelings were all over the map. Pride. Outrage. Connection to the land and the people. And then shame. Shame welled up in me with the voice of an angry relative. It was as if both the prosecutor and the accused were living inside the court of my own mind. I felt the shame of being brought out into the open and being charged with living in a culture that is responsible for so much pain. At the same time, I felt I was one of the many who had been robbed, beaten, and, worse, assimilated. The culture of my ancestors was being faded out by the bright lights of the next thing for sale in the consumer world of today.

I felt conflicted, saddened, and confused, as I had many times before over the years, as I had tried again and again to find my place, and myself, within the mixture of my ancestors. Letting the tobacco fall to the ground and roll in the wind, I turned to all four directions and asked myself, *Was I related to this, too?*

Returning to the van, and heading closer to town, we approached the residential area of the reservation. There, the reality of an entirely different scene flooded my weary eyes. Against the majestic backdrop of the Northern Arizona mountains, decaying, rusted-out cars, trash, and broken glass lay strewn in the backyards of some residents. The contrast was startling, and I was forced to turn within to find the beauty in this situation. What I was seeing was a sign of the decay that the Western culture has brought to these lands and the confusion it has brought to people living there. The abandonment of what was deemed no longer useful was painful for me to witness.

Then I started to see myself in it. I realized that at some point it would be me lying there, under the elements, season after season, from the first snow to the blazing heat of the Arizona summer. I will be returned to the earth, discarded, and no longer useful, as my unwitting purpose will have been served. As my mind spun with those ideas, I realized that I could be disposed of even before that final moment.

Today, in our contemporary culture, we seem to be valued for little more than the jobs we fulfill. Then, when we're no longer capable of doing that job, being productive in some way, or no longer considered of service to society, we are thrown into a no-man's-land to be disposed of. So many of us will be placed in retirement communities, mental hospitals, and prisons where we're no longer privileged enough to interact with "productive" and "normal" society.

As I gazed at the decaying life around me, it struck me that it was not a sign of laziness or a sign of a lack of discipline, which we are led to believe it is. That is not the way of the *Dineh*. That is not the truth here.

No, in this place, a symptom of the country's consumerism was rearing its ugly head. Even in this remote land, the confusion borne by the *Western illusion* is felt. For the people of the land, the rusting cars symbolize that confusion as they lie unwanted and unloved even in our most remote tribes. I began to see the rusty cars and the out of place trash as an artistic expression of a rebellion against a consumerist system of single-use packaging and superficial products—a system of production for the means of consumption.

I wondered why we don't go ahead and make the ugliness of this flaw in human behavior more visible. Why not show what decay looks like, after all? Maybe it is more honest to leave it in bold relief.

In our contemporary society, we get intoxicated with media, work, school, and thousands of other distractions that captivate us. It's a dangerous addiction. America is walking the plank of social, environmental, and cultural destruction. Sadly, most people don't get the privilege of seeing the decay in such bold relief. Instead, America does what she has done with free people for hundreds of years: send them to places where that freedom is neatly packaged into a market-friendly consumer message. America has taken the culture of sovereignty, freedom, and wildness of the human spirit and put it out of sight, burying it in the landfill of our own distortions.

All Americans face this challenge nowadays. Some of us hide our trash better than others; some of us have huge machines that make enormous holes in *Mother Earth* in which to bury it. The scale of consumption in the U.S. is so recent and so invasive that Native American peoples have their own systems to deal with it just like the rest of us. For some *Dineh*, the garbage is laid out and displayed right in front for any traveler like me to see. The rusty cars, the abandoned couches, mattresses, and debris were a reminder of the devastation that the Western ways have brought to the world. They boldly declared that the consumption of our cultural identity is literally destroying everything in its path. For some of *Dineh* of the land, the broken-down cars and the trash strewn around may have represented a sign of rebellion from the materialism of the culture around them. In the cluster of the rez, it was a sign of disconnection from the material. It was exactly what drew so many of us to the ways of the *Navajo* in the first place.

My internal dialogue then morphed into understanding. I recognized that, as the wheels of consumerism and consumption spin through the reservation—as it knocks on the doors of the people here, threatening their spiritual, social, economic, and health traditions, and their very way of being—the people fight. They fight through contaminated water and smoke-filled skies. They fight from archaic, underfunded coal-burning electrical plants. They fight through poverty, assimilation, genocide, and racism. These relatives of mine fight to protect and preserve their way of life.

***

At the Gathering of Healers, I had met Philmore Bluehouse, who personally invited me to attend a small ceremony in his family *Hogan*. So, there I was, sitting in an ancestral home, being warmed by the fire and by the hearts of a group of people I didn't really know. We were all seekers and we sat quietly waiting for something to happen. I sat to the right of our host. I watched the fire burn. I ran my fingers across the dirt floor feeling the Earth beneath me. It was all so beautiful to me, as if a doorway to the past had opened. I begin to realize how special the opportunity was before me.

I began to think about the *Hogan* further. It seemed designed to focus the energy in the middle of the home, to build family and community, and to share teachings. It consisted of one room where families would work and live together and where communities could congregate. It had no hidden corners and no places where someone might be left out. Every part of the lives of those who lived in this humble home seemed to have a meaning and purpose that would be easy to miss if you only look at the surface.

And then the introductions began.

I didn't know that the spoken words of a simple introduction would take hold of me and start to formulate within me a deeper understanding of my own self-identity. I hadn't had the privilege of understanding those kinds of things yet. I had not grown up in a traditional Native American home. But through the encounter in that hogan, I discovered the magic, borne from an introduction, that can deeply enhance the human experience.

One by one, several elders introduced themselves. It wasn't that they needed to say much. It was that they wanted to introduce themselves to the group. They wanted to speak their clans along with the identity of the people that they descended from. There was a perceptible sense of magic that fortified them inside the process. It seemed to me that when they introduced themselves, their backs straightened and their gaze intensified. It felt like they created a spiritual identity. As they did so, an infinite understanding of this ancient technology began to take root in my own heart.

A *Navajo* woman, an elder, spoke of the lands that her ancestors came from. She introduced herself using the traditional clan method. She spoke her family identity in a certain, precise order: she spoke her mother's clan, her father's clan, her mother's father, and her father's father. She identified herself with a deep lineage of people that went back thousands of years. I was astonished at the level of understanding she had of who she was. I was amazed at how fluidly she spoke of her people and how she was powerful in the way of understanding.

Was I ready to embark on a journey that would help me come to grips with my own ancestry, in my own contemporary life? More questions began to arise in my mind. I wanted to learn more about what the power of this ceremonial introduction meant to me. I wanted to understand more about what it meant to be indigenous. As simple as it seemed, I wanted to understand how to introduce myself in my own way. I felt I had missed something growing up—that an important part of me had been disconnected from myself, my family, my community and the planet. It was a void that I didn't know even existed until I witnessed the power of these relatives using their wisdom of self to claim their power and to be comfortable with that knowing.

As we sat listening, a woman entered the *Hogan* with a dog. One of the elders remarked that the dog needed to be taken out of the *hogan*, but Philmore graciously said the dog could stay. With that, I realized that Philmore was more than just your average Native American teacher. His actions and his response to the dog spoke to me. My heart felt open to him; in him, I felt a kindred spirit. I had the sense that what he was about to share with us was more than just a single tradition; I felt that what I was about to receive would change my life. Little did I know at the time that what was being shared would go on to change the lives of countless people from around the world.

He began the ceremony by introducing himself. He spoke of the clans he was associated with; he told us of the lands that his ancestors had come from; he talked about his direct connection to the *Anasazi*, the people who came before. I call this a *technology of identity*. It provides so much more than our usual understanding of our identity as we know it in our contemporary lives. Since my first encounter with this language in the *Hogan* that night, I've sat with many elders in sweat lodge ceremony and listened to them talk about themselves with a tremendously vast sense of self-identity. It's not just about identifying who you are born from and who you were born to, it is also about recognizing that your lines go back directly to the lands from which your ancestors emerged.

Witnessing this tribal introduction, so many questions came to my mind. Questions about myself and questions about my origin. I know that within my DNA, there's a story of my Native American heritage and that I have a genetic connection to the land. *But how much of it has been lost? Did my ancestors know the exact mountain on which my ancient tribal grandmas and grandpas gave birth to our family line? What happened to this knowledge of who we are? What happened to our connection to the land? Why was it taken from me and so many others like me? Why was this information no longer a part of my life and my daughter's life?*

***

I believe that for any child growing up in this culture with the story of being Native American there is huge reckoning that has to take place. It's a conflict that each of us must come to grips with; the denial of that story only fosters unresolved issues. The Native American story encompasses so much loss. Too much has been taken from us; we have experienced too much pain. So many have been displaced and misunderstood. So much needs to be restored, regenerated, and re-processed in a way that can serve us in our daily lives of navigating contemporary culture. Yet our losses can help us to transmute that energy into something that serves us. What we've lost and what we do have resonates inside of anyone who has the courage to look at their life, and what they and the ancestors have sacrificed, and make a choice not to further foster submission to a culture of denial and dismissal.

I could have stayed comfortable in my modern life as just another American. I have always been able to fit in with almost every group of the contemporary melting pot of American society when I want to and learning to navigate race and culture has always been one of my survival skills. And although racism has never felt good to me, it has been a part of my life; it is something that I have had to think about many times in many places. Sadly, I think for most Americans this is the truth of living in this country. Although, I have been told of people that just live in denial of the truth of racism, it is still a part of growing honest with yourself and learning to evolve as humans.

I have felt the separation from many sides of my mixed cultural identity. And for me, the process of going into this place of culture and race is about leaving the comfortable and asking the real, hard questions. It would be much easier to simply kneel down to an "American identity" — an identity constructed and molded in the mines, fields, and sales departments of the global marketplace of consumerism. But I can also courageously ask myself, *If I am indigenous, what does that feel like?*

These internal struggles were brought to the surface of my heart as I sat there on the cold ground of the reservation in an ancient ceremonial *Hogan*. I began to understand that I could speak my genetic connection to my Native American lands while embracing the lands of my European heritage at the same time. I began to understand that the land *itself* gives birth to my identity.

Philmore continued his powerful introduction, stating that he was related to *Anasazi*, an extremely ancient people. He spoke of their blood being his blood and made the point that genetic links are only part of the story. And at that point, I began to grasp the idea that there's more to an introduction than just the words: *Hello, my name is Andrew and I play the drum*. There, at the end of my introduction, inside the container of ceremony, is a process that can fortify one's deepest spiritual makeup.

As I shared space with my *Dineh* relatives, I initiated a journey of education and self-realization that would span many years. It would bring me a deep understanding of my identity and the foundation of my truest self. It would empower me to let go of the self-created identities that don't serve me, to understand and embrace them in the process, and to ultimately open myself to the wisdom, clarity, and guidance of my ancestors and the profound spiritual truth that I am.

CHAPTER 2

A SACRED INTRODUCTION

Hello, I am Andrew Ecker. My mother Kathy Lindsey. My father Dale Ecker. My mother's mother Elva Gallegos, Apache woman from New Mexico. My father's mother, Evelyn Beatty, an Irish woman from Pennsylvania. My mother's father, Leroy Lindsey, an Apache man from Arkansas. And my father's father, Wayne Ecker, Algonquin and German from Pennsylvania.

This simple introduction has become the basis of what I call *The Sacred 7*, or *The Seven Sacred Containers of Self-Identity*. To me, this introduction comprises a powerful spiritual and energetic truth about a person. It expresses the foundation of the human experience in a relational manner, and for me, reflects what I know myself to be. This introduction does not bring up what I can do for you or how we can build a business together or how we can make money together. Instead, very simply, it gives a foundation to connect and relate to each other. Without the basic understanding that it offers to me, all the other parts of myself as a human being exist without strength, fortitude, or depth. It connects me to the Earth and to the gifts that generations before me have passed on to me in this life. It is also a doorway to the expansion of my own eternal existence, to the source of tremendous wisdom and direction, and to the means to experience a life that is more free, more loving, and more abundant.

The Sacred 7 introduction is a sacred ceremonial practice that has been a prominent thread in the fabric of tribal communities for thousands of years. It has been invoked in some version during ceremonies and spoken to present visitors to a group in the community. By invoking *The Sacred 7*, people have been honoring their families, honoring themselves, deepening their connection to their history and to the Earth, and feeding their deepest spiritual identity.

As I have journeyed with the medicine of this tool of spirituality, it has given me insight into its pragmatic power. In the technology of ceremonial introduction and identity, I have found a new freedom to choose what brings life to me. It has shaken away the chains of the identities that have been thrust upon me and that I willingly suited up with for many years. It has been a light in the darkness for me and a blanket of protection and humility from the blinding light of my own emerging egoic self-inflated wisdom.

A SACRED INTRODUCTION

You might notice that my introduction above contains no verbs. There are no 'is' or 'was' in the telling of my *Sacred 7*, for those words would limit its scope and focus. Like the whole of *The Sacred 7* technology, the introduction requires you to think in a nonlinear way, revealing the profound depth underneath the surface act of naming the names of one's lineage. It's not for your mind to grasp the particulars and analyze the pieces of the whole. It's for your heart to bring forth the presence of your forebears and your own existence all at once.

In *The Sacred 7* introduction, you name the seven sacred souls who, in the *Pre-Existence*, made an agreement to come forward and manifest as you. These seven souls are energetic *containers* because they hold space for you, embrace you, and weave their purpose and energetic signature into your heart. They come through your lineage and embrace you as they inform who you are. Ultimately, they become you at the most profound level. They are your medicine.

The containers of *The Sacred 7* are you, your mother, your father, your mother's mother, your father's mother, your mother's father, and your father's father. Each one of these perspectives of self is an individual aspect relating to the whole and has a teaching and a deep meaning. These *Sacred 7* bring the totality of life into intentional focus and enables you to find your power and medicine for the world. It fosters the discovery of your identity and purpose. This sacred agreement was forged in an existence that is beyond the linear concepts of time and space. And so, in the unwinding of the ceremonial introduction, there is a story that describes how you came to be.

The Sacred 7 honors the feminine. This is done by introducing your mother and ending with the father's father and when introducing the women, we use the names they were born with, not their married names. This is because mothers and grandmothers were whole and complete on their own. In our contemporary life, we are attached to our father's father name without any mention of the wombs that gave us life. *The Sacred 7* brings back the power of the feminine side of our life by acknowledging this part of who we are. It helps us return our feminine and masculine aspects back to balance after being subjected to living in this culture.

Each of the containers represents and calls on the expanse of your consciousness within each of the seven directions. You, as the inward direction, representing the inner child. Your mother represents the space below, *Mother Earth*, and the divine feminine. Your father represents the space above, the Divine Masculine, as we think of *Father Sky*. Your mother's mother lies in the East and represents new relationships while your father's mother is found in the South, embodying your relationship to your family. Your mother's father is in the West, symbolizing who you are to the community. Lastly, your father's father in the North represents you in your relationship with the elements and everything they govern: the animals, the star nations, the trees, the air, water, fire, earth, gravity, time and spirit.

Honoring the seven directions gives us a more expansive view of our identity, allowing us to loosen ourselves from our singular, hyper-focused, limited perceptions. The seven directions offer a multiplicity of perspectives from which we gain freedom and higher wisdom. For example, if I was limited to only one perspective, say, from the East, it would be easy for me to see only the failures, poor choices and breakdowns of my life. However, if I turn and see myself from the direction of the West—representing who I

A SACRED INTRODUCTION

am to my community—I get a whole new view. I see the broken child trying to find love. I see my desperate need for an accepting, loving family and I remember those in my neighborhood who encouraged my innocent younger self to make poor, self-destructive choices. Through *The Sacred 7*, I get an expansive understanding of myself that encompasses the many facets of my truth.

With this understanding of the sacred agreement and preexistence of the eternal soul, I have learned to experience much more than just the family members in my lineage and what their roles implies. I have evolved to see my personal lessons and medicine embodied in physical form. I have looked into the infinite space of *Spirit* and seen the hand of *Source Creator God* in the face of my grandmother. I felt her speak to me, through the nonlinear halls of eternal presence, saying, *I will bear a child named Kathy. I will be the mother of a young girl who will suffer through the disease of drug addiction. I will be her mother, and I will go to the jails and pay the bail for her. I will wait up for her late at night. I have the strength to incarnate in this powerful role.*

I have learned that my own mother, a flawed, wounded, life-long drug addict, gave me a gift of understanding, acceptance, and unconditional love. Her pain of being unable to stop the cycle of addiction and the disease of mental illness has led me to a deep place of recognition within myself. It manifests itself any time I look into the eyes of an addict or a child of an incarcerated or drug addicted parent and hear within myself, *I know you. I know your pain. I have lived through it, too.* In these connections and revelations, I find great medicine and reconciliation of my life that gives me purpose and gifts to give to others.

With that understanding as a backdrop, I reasoned

with life and found a story that serves me. I have felt into the suffering and seen into the pain and awakened to a truth that my grandmother chose to be my grandmother. She chose to give birth to my mother, and she made an agreement that would help lead her to a greater understanding of who she is. In turn, my mother chose to experience many things, including suffering from drug addiction, so she could learn the medicine of empathy, and so I could too. The gifts of each life are passed on to the next for self-discovery and soul evolution. This idea can transport you and give meaning and purpose to all that you do.

Just as importantly, we do not just passively receive the gifts that are passed on to us from previous generations. Each of us generates an agreement and makes choices of our own in the *Pre-Existence*. In my case, I chose to come into this life with two parents who suffered from drug addiction, a mixed-race background, and numerous life experiences that would elevate my spiritual path and provide me the medicine to recognize and transform who I am.

***

Quite the opposite from *The Sacred 7*, our contemporary world teaches us to find our identity within the careers we choose, the neighborhood we grow up in, our roles in other people's lives, our likes and dislikes, and what other people tell us about ourselves. We like to think we know who we are and we recount our training, history, accomplishments, life goals, and successes and failures just to prove it. *"What do you do?"* is a favorite early question for people to begin

A SACRED INTRODUCTION

to know each other. We let these few factors of our lives limit who we know ourselves to be as individuals. They are but superficial understandings of who we are as deep and expansive souls.

Over time, we learn to be comfortable and even loyal to the safety within this captivity of identity. Our cultural programming and the limitations of language teach us to define what is good and bad, right and wrong. Still, underneath the surface of that complacency, many of us feel that something is missing or askew, and we justifiably ask what is wrong. Some go on searching for the next cure to fix themselves—a goal that is rarely fulfilled. The power of our prison of identity keeps us disconnected, confused, and often lost. As we live within the constructs and limitations that come along with our cultural identities, something very important within us is cut off from reach.

Consider my story. I have survived heroin, cocaine, alcohol addiction, and attempted suicide. I have known myself as an addict, a felon, a criminal, an entrepreneur, a Christian, an Apache, a Buddhist, a White Man, a Mexican, a Chicano, a father, a son, a boyfriend, a husband, a warrior, a peacemaker, a gangster, a student, and a saint. I have been kept captive within a conceptual identity of prophet, healer, athlete, preacher, yogi, and loser. To name a few. Yet, these titles of identity war amongst themselves and bring confusion and disconnection. They limit what is possible for my joy and service to the planet.

They provide only a fractured view of myself, not a quantum viewpoint of my whole self. While only seeing myself as a felon or a warrior, I don't see the whole of my blessed life. I don't get the quantum viewpoint, and as a result, I am imprisoned right within my own body, mind, and self.

The Sacred 7 can give you a new way to define yourself that can bring clarity, connection, and freedom. It is both ancient and pragmatic. Within its sacred technology, you tap into an identity that provides expansion and freedom rather than the captivity of the identity that your culture assumes for you. It is a way to break the chains and release the bonds of your own constructs.

***

Diving into the reality of *The Sacred 7 Containers* requires us to explore the *metaphysical architecture* of our identity—the conceptual environment and building blocks of who we know ourselves to be. Your *metaphysical architecture* works in *symbiosis* with the *subatomic frequency* —the place where your thoughts and consciousness become matter—to manifest and reveal what you are connected to, what serves you, and what service you can bring to the planet. It is a pliable and fortified energetic dimension where your choices can decide what building blocks you will build onto and what vibration you will resonate with.

If you don't explore the *metaphysical architecture* from which most of your life is spawned, you are simply, unconsciously, captive to this energy. For me, the energetic building blocks of my identity were laid down in my childhood, slapped in place by the school I attended, the times I lived in, my family, and more. I actually remember the time and place when I first began to be aware of it entering my space like a tangible presence. It was as if I was being encased in a robe of energy and captivity, like putting the chains on that would forever keep me in place. That was when I became certain of my identity as a drug-addict-in-the-making and a criminal with a scripted future.

A SACRED INTRODUCTION

From then on, I saw that people held me in that space and I soon learned that I often contained myself in it, too. It was a fortified, yet distorted, energetic field that was so tangible to me that at times I would see my behavior and think, *Man, you are an addict, a real criminal. You're a nightmare.*

Many years later, I became more conscious of the power of energy and how our thought creates reality. This drew me to become a student of the power of *metaphysical architecture* and to explore the boundaries of self through music, prayer, and meditation. As my awareness of it grew, I recognized *metaphysical architecture* for what it is: a doorway to true freedom beyond our usual concepts of existence. After all, how do we define freedom? The word is resounding in our rhetoric these days, as factions argue about their rights and freedoms in this country and debate about their interpretations of the First and Second Amendments of the U.S. Constitution. We get used to defining freedom as something that our governments and institutions bestow upon us or take away. Ironically, putting the power in their hands in that way disempowers us and leaves us without choice concerning our own freedom. Ultimately, we give up our sovereignty, lose our truest freedom, and see in ourselves little more than what we do to make money.

True freedom is an inner, spiritual state; not something that can be thrust upon you or taken away. Freedom gives you the ability to see yourself with compassion and to observe your suffering and pain and see it as medicine. True freedom comes from a sense of emotional sovereignty or the ability to transcend emotional captivity. When I took drugs, I did it as a way to control my emotions. Years of living with violence, instability, and neglect left me with little or no freedom from my own suffering. PTSD had robbed me of peace; heroin, alcohol, cocaine, and meth were giving me a new feeling, a ceremony ritual, and even a peer group that accepted me. The drugs filled the void and gave me a false sense of control that later took control of me. In the midst of my full-on addiction, I had no emotional sovereignty; I had no real freedom from my pain, anger, frustration, and fear. None. Even though I was physically autonomous, there were times when I would barricade myself into hotels rooms and sometimes my own house, trying to find a safe space to reconcile my childhood trauma, my adult addiction, and years of toxic identity. There was no escape because what I was running from were unseen viral processes downloaded unconsciously and accepted in the illusion of my self-identity. I would shut out anyone who wanted to get near me. As a captive of my past, even as the years progressed, I perpetuated my own addiction and criminal behavior.

Even with that seeming life sentence, the magic of *The Sacred 7* gave me a true path to emotional sovereignty and a freedom that I could never have conceived of previously.

***

It is time now for all of humanity to discover that who we are as individuals is not what we do or what we feel or what pain and suffering we have passed through. Those are merely fragments of the whole of what we are. Now is the time for more and more of us to open our inner being to a deeper experience of ourselves. There is a part of us that is patiently waiting to be revealed, and it is accessible with the help of *The Sacred 7*. By discovering it, we unleash what it means to be truly alive.

CHAPTER 3

SEEDS OF DESTINY

Late one night, when I was about eleven years old, the front door to my family's home exploded with noise. Five police officers had forced open the door and rushed into our small three-bedroom home in southeast Portland. With guns drawn and flashlights blinding my eyes, they screamed commands at us. I had been asleep on the couch, lulled to sleep by the shimmering lights of our Christmas tree. The officers said they had a warrant for my mother's arrest. Apparently, she had evaded them many times before by escaping out a window, climbing down a tree, and running to my uncle's house. They were going to search the place, as usual, they said and they weren't going to leave without her.

I had experienced raids before, but this night forever changed me. When the police found my mom, they brought her down the stairs while I sat on the couch in tears, trembling in fear with my sister and grandma. My mom screamed and struggled, kicking and protesting as three officers threw her to the ground, lifting and pushing her back down over and over again. We watched in horror, petrified in fear. My mom screamed at the police officers only to have them get more violent. Just over five feet tall, she was fighting like a caged animal, just wanting to say goodbye to us. I remember her long brown hair over her face. I remember the fear of watching the person that I considered to be my protector defeated and beaten in her own home.

War seems to always come home at some point. When it does, it comes unbidden, traumatically, and suddenly. Before the raid, my house had been the place where I laughed and played games. It had been the place where my grandma cooked tortillas and made the chili Verde, the place where she prayed with me. It was the place my mom, with all of her toughness, and my grandpa, the military guardian of our family, taught me to be the man of the house. It was the place where all the protectors of my life could be found.

Yet within that safety, there was calamity. My parents' lives revolved around their cocaine and heroin dependency. It was their downfall and their medicine at the same time, because without it, they would not survive. They paid for their medicine dearly—with their freedom, security, integrity, acceptance & ultimately their lives. Their way of paying for their medicine was to steal in ways that they could maintain and justify. All things considered, life didn't offer them many choices; the tragedy of their drug addiction robbed them of that. My mom and dad seemed to have a special talent for shoplifting and honed the craft into an art. As I got older, they'd tell me stories of those who had gone before them, the many "boosts" that they had committed, spinning proud tales of their conquests and their wisdom. Our friends and neighbors called my mom and dad *boosters*—a name that commanded a certain respect. After all, boosters weren't like the common "junkies" you heard about in the news, the ones who seemed to be so quickly blamed for virtually every crime committed. Boosters were not street prostitutes, armed robbers, or the kids stealing from their own families. Boosters followed a code of integrity. They took care of the neighborhood; they only stole from stores, never from people.

To many of us, my parents and others like them were on a warrior's path, fighting the fight, and finding the means to survive in an unjust and unfair world. Even more than that, the lifestyle of a booster had an aura of sovereignty, strength and freedom. If they were any good, they'd work in crews of two to eight people, depending on what the target was. The tribe mentality meant you'd always have someone watching your back; on the street, those without a crew became isolated and later victims of the loneliness and the predators that were a part of that world.

The culture and friendships that my parents enjoyed within the harshness, brutality, and human degradation of the drug culture created a nest of safety that appeared to be elevated above the lives of everyone else blindly complying with America's lopsided system of greed. The stores themselves were the expression of this culture of consumerism, a culture that was diametrically opposed to ours. Within the drug culture, we were a tribe, we helped each other out when a need arose. We were a family, regardless of the blood within our veins. For those who lived a lifetime without knowing comfort and acceptance, this culture provided it. I think what most don't understand about that culture is that for so many it serves deep needs within the individual.

My mom often said, *I can't believe that people pay this much for these things! I can't believe that they have the balls to charge people that much money*! She told me that corporations were ripping people off, so, heck, we were doing the right thing by ripping off the corporations in return.

In my young child's mind, the culture I grew up in had an identity that defined it. To me, we were just Like the Native Americans they called "savages" in the John Wayne movies I watched as a kid. We were like roaming bands of renegade Indians, raiding department stores for the greater good of keeping ourselves and our cultural identity alive. Ours was a violent, distorted, and self-destructive counter-cultural movement, an ideology that fed on itself—but it was worth everything to us. It also identified our enemies for us, namely, the institutions, jails, prisons, hospitals, police, and prosecutors, and anyone else who judged and condemned us.

The city of my birth, Southeast Portland, Oregon, was a unique place. It looked like a couple of Volkswagen buses and some Harley-Davidsons had broken down at the same unfortunate location and their frustrated owners decided to build a tree house and call it home. With districts like Hawthorne and neighborhoods like Felony Flats, it was a colorful place to live. Tie-dyed Grateful Dead posters and rainbow flags hung in the windows. Bikes were parked in front. Most of my friends and their parents openly smoked marijuana. It was just a part of the counterculture. Around the neighborhood, the front yards hinted at unsuccessful attempts at gardening. The homeless were usually dressed in camouflage, leftovers from the Vietnam War. Several shops on the streets were closed but the easy business of selling liquor and cigarettes remained a part of the Portland way of life.

    While my family had a loose relationship with this vaguely hippy culture, we didn't exactly fit in. We were a brown family in a white neighborhood and in the midst of all the drugs, alcohol, violence, and craziness there was a feeling of traditional values. My Grandma Elva taught me to pray when I was very young, and she made great meals with thick, homemade tortillas that didn't last on the table for very long. My grandfather Leroy drank away the pain of 23 years in the military, he took the time to explain to me who I was from behind a bottle of Wild Turkey whiskey. Although my mother lived with me, it was really my grandparents who raised me. When I was four years old, my parents divorced and my father moved to Arizona.

    Some of my earliest memories are of going to grocery stores with my mom to help her boost. I'd be her lookout. I'd stand in the shopping cart, facing her, and look over her shoulder to see if anyone was watching. When I would tell her the coast was clear, she'd stuff some goods into a diaper bag or her purse. Sometimes, she would shove things in her coat or the waistband of the pantyhose she had worn just for the occasion. Whatever way she could get the goods to the car, she would.

    Life was filled with both excitement and fear. It seemed like we were always running from someone, conspiring to do something and for some reason I loved every minute of it. I'd even cry when my mom went without me. Whether she was boosting or buying drugs, it didn't matter. I wanted to be with her. For within that eye of the hurricane of drug addiction, abuse and crime that encircled us there was a tremendous bond between us.. I knew that even in the chaotic mess of life—while I was sometimes neglected and sometimes abused—I was never without love.

Though the police were a source of great trauma for me, they were not the only source of it. Growing up in that kind of culture, violence was a part of life, whether from a family member or the street. When I was in the third grade, my uncle beat me until I was lying in a fetal position in the bathtub, blood coming out of my nose, my head throbbing in pain. Later, I understood that it was the only way he knew to try to protect and love me. He was a former marine and he had been abused as a child himself. In his sick, alcoholic, and distorted way, he was doing what he thought was right: beating me up to try and teach me not to steal.

Yet, within the complexities of a child's mind, I defended and protected him. Once, he beat me so bad that both my eyes were black. When my mom came home and asked how it happened, I told her that I was jumped by a couple of Vietnamese boys on the playground. What I didn't tell her was that my uncle had caught me stealing from my grandma to bankroll a quick trip to the video arcade up the street from our house. I had seen my mom's intensely violent side a couple of times and I'd do anything to avoid it. I didn't want to tell her about my culpability.

Instead, for the next hour, my mom put me in the car and we drove around the neighborhood looking for the perpetrators of the crime. She stopped the car to talk with one of the fences she did business with. He was a bootlegger. In Portland back then, you could not buy alcohol on Sunday, so there was a whole subculture of bootleggers who sold stolen alcohol and cigarettes. This guy was particularly mean and colorful. He was filthy, constantly smoking cigarettes, always had a gun within reach, and held some sort of machine to his throat so he could talk. He looked at me sitting in the car, with my black and blue face, and said, *Man, those Gooks fucked him up.* Then he handed my mom a towel with something in it. I asked her what it was and she told me to just watch the street for those punks. I knew then that she was willing to really hurt someone. For what seemed like a lifetime, we resumed our mission to find my fictitious Vietnamese boys.

In those days, I kept a pretty cool exterior, but the internal pressure I was feeling was intense and traumatizing. I didn't feel like anyone knew what I was living with on the inside. I was surviving in a big, angry world that seemed to hate our family and I was filled with anxiety and fear. My mom repeatedly warned me that the police would take me away if we got caught boosting. On simple drives to the store, she'd yell out, *You kids hide in the back!* because she had spotted a police officer; of course, we were never buckled in. From then on, any time I saw a police officer, I'd go into a panic. My heart would start racing just from the sound of sirens screaming in the street.

My grandmother passed away not long after the raid; the struggles of raising my sister and me in combination with dealing with my mom were too much for her. Life changed for everyone in my family after she passed from this existence. It became even more complicated as my sister and I were sent away to stay with different family members. For the next seven years, I was always uncertain where I would live next.

I was an intelligent kid, too. During story time in school, I'd stand in front of the class and talk about the animals and places that were mentioned in the stories that were being read to us. I'd embellish with what I'd learned from my grandfather's stories from his ventures around the world. Yet on the inside, I was an emotional wreck. I was waking up in the middle of the night and going on perimeter checks. I was cutting myself, burning myself, going to the bathroom on myself. There were times when I was actually paralyzed with fear.

Today, we are finally learning that all of the behaviors I exhibited back then are typical in children who have experienced the kinds of traumas I lived through. As symptoms of *Post-Traumatic Stress Disorder* (PTSD), they remain somewhat elusive to treat by traditional methods.

Those with PTSD have a strong desire to take control of their surroundings and I was no different. When I was twelve years old, I was given an opportunity to heal in a unique way. Like much of my life, I now see these events as the *Hand of Providence* at work for my greater good. It was then that I was sent to stay with my Native American grandfather, Leroy Lindsey, in the middle of the Ozark Mountains in Arkansas. He was a 23-year career military war veteran who initiated me into a completely different way of life. He lived in a shack home with a tin roof and only intermittent running water, and through him, I was introduced to the land and to a simpler, more direct way of living. I learned to hunt, fish, farm, and trap. Somehow, within the security and safety of that environment, far away from the sirens of the city, I calmed down. I even taught myself to go to the bathroom on my own.

This one change in my behavior was a huge accomplishment and source of pride for me. For so many years, I had lived with the shame of my lack of control. My family never talked about it. They'd just send me to the laundry room to clean my soiled clothes, saved for me in a bucket of bleach and water, which would inevitably burn my hands. Even worse, sometimes they'd make me wear adult diapers. So, even as I tried to enjoy myself on outings to the zoo, Disneyland, and other fun places with other kids, I'd often be walking around in soiled underclothes, ashamed, and thoroughly miserable.

In those mountains of Arkansas, I found a new connection to the land, to my own body, and to a natural rhythm that supported me. I was starting to learn that I had some choices in life.

***

The police raid on my family's home was a shock to my body and my spirit. It riddled my childhood with a sense of perpetual violence and powerlessness. It robbed me of my innocence. When the police finished their search for drugs after the raid and let the rest of us back in the house, I felt like I walked into a different world. The Christmas presents weren't under the tree anymore; they had been torn open with bits of wrapping paper tossed everywhere. Sofa cushions where unzipped; the mattresses upstairs were cut open; clothes were thrown all over the place. It felt as if a vengeance had been launched against us and that something was intent on ripping apart and destroying my family, my home, and my life.

I often wondered why the police were so brutal to my family and me that night. *Was it because my Spanish-speaking, Native American grandmother answered the door, so they had to beat up my mom and throw her to the ground in front of my sister and me? Maybe her five-foot frame and dark brown features threatened their sensibilities of what Portland residents were supposed to look like? Or maybe they didn't like the smell of our traditional food cooking in the kitchen?*

It could also have something to do with the acrid smell of hatred set ablaze by the political climate of the so-called *War on Drugs* of that time. The issue had been a constant and successful theme for people who were trying to get elected to public office. Newcomers to the field could easily jump on the bandwagon and win some points by breaking up families and hauling them off to prison. Then the nation got in a frenzy pointing fingers at the substance abusers who were poisoning their idyllic American way. President Ronald Reagan was talking about quelling the storm of illegal drugs and locking up *those horrible people* who were at the root of the problem. At the same time, deep cuts were made to federal mental health grants. The public got strung along and finally seemed to agree that all crime stemmed from drug users like my mom and dad. It was simply not true. People who use drugs don't commit serious crimes. There's research to back that up now. Some addicts shoplift and some sell drugs to supply their drug habit and to survive to the next day. They are hardly the horrible people causing the ills in society.

Meanwhile, in the streets, the *War on Drugs* seemed a thinly veiled attempt to give police the right to bully people they didn't like or understand. They weren't helping anybody, just hurting us. It seemed that they wanted to persecute us without cause. It was devastating and I felt the fallout from it throughout my childhood and well into my adult life.

***

SEEDS OF DESTINY

The cold love of heroin was the foundation of my parents' love for each other. They used to smuggle heroin across the border from Tijuana into San Diego together. I'm told that my mother had a unique talent for swallowing a few balloons of heroin and regurgitating them once they were across the border. In those days, the Mexican heroin dealers didn't use scales; they only used large silver spoons to measure each take. A simple press of the hands and the portion would be calculated perfectly. My dad told me that when they got back to the U.S. and measured the stash on the triple beam scale, they were almost always perfect.

My father later told me that my mom had no fear of the heroin in her body. She wouldn't even think twice about it. Just knowing that she could die sometimes made him nauseous when he would watch her getting ready to swallow those balloons. At some point, my dad's fear and his love for my mother outweighed the score and they left San Diego for Portland, Oregon.

When I was five or six years old, I was told that I had a father I didn't know about; my memory of him from my younger years had faded completely away. My family told me that he lived in Arizona and they were going to send me to go visit him. Even though he had lived with us when I was very young, I had no memory of him, so the idea that he existed was a revelation to me. Arizona could have been as far away as Mars, as far as I was concerned. Yet, when I heard about the journey there, I felt like some unclaimed part of myself had been coaxed awake; a spark of self-reflection was lit.

It was a huge culture shock for me to leave my home in verdant Portland, and its comfortable dysfunction, to be flown out to visit a whole new world in the desert. For five years, starting when I was in the first grade, I was shipped to the Phoenix area every summer to visit my father and then shipped back to Portland for the school year. I started to play with kids that actually looked like me: Chicano, Mexican American, Native American. We lived in a small house in Peoria, Arizona, a predominantly Mexican American neighborhood. It was a lower middle-class community that looked rich from my battered young eyes. From predictable meal times to cloth napkins, there were differences that were a bit confusing to me at first. Ironically, the race equation had turned on its head: now my people were considered a white family in a brown neighborhood, and once again we had to try to figure out how to fit in.

Most people in the area were good hard-working people. The nuclear plant employed three families on our street and it was a decent neighborhood but there was enough of a drug culture for my dad to stay busy. He even seemed to have made a name for himself in the criminal world there. The Mexican Mafia there called him *Robin Hood* out of the respect he had gained over the years in service to this culture. He stole from the rich and then sold to the poor for only half the price. Even the folks coming out of church on Sundays couldn't resist the deals my dad offered for juicy steaks, men's cologne, and small electronics.

In those early days in Arizona, I had a pretty good relationship with my dad. He'd do his best to spend time with me and I really loved him. We'd play video games, eat pizza, go to the movies, or even watch the WWF in the stadium. But inevitably, before or after we spent time together, he'd have to have his "medicine."

My dad didn't get me to help him steal goods until I was a lot older. He did, however, take me to drug houses with him frequently where I would wait for him while he got high. We'd go to some dirty, cockroach-infested shack in Northwest Phoenix that sold drugs, held cockfights, and dealt in stolen merchandise. My dad would take me around and show off his little brown son. I remember nodding when he told everyone that my mom was Mexican even though she wasn't. She had been born in Las Vegas on a military base and didn't even speak fluent Spanish, but it seemed important to him to say that. Of course, I didn't know any better, so I just nodded and went along with it. It was always a frightening experience for me, which I never quite got used to it. Even if there were other kids in the home, they were usually bullies of some sort. I often sat on the floor, entertaining myself as best I could, while I waited for hours and hours.

From visiting drug houses with my dad, to helping my mom steal cigarettes, to witnessing the drug raids and the violence that our people endured, I was being trained into a culture of crime. I must have acquired a college degree's worth of education in crime during those years, serving as a rite of passage in my father's eyes. Even so, I had to prove myself many times on the streets. I was right on the verge of anchoring into my mind the very identity I most wanted to avoid.

***

When I was in the fifth grade the cultural war came to my school in Portland. Shortly after I returned from visiting my father's family in Arizona, and just before the night my mom was beaten in front of me by the police, the Nancy Reagan D.A.R.E. officers arrived at our school, armed with banners and badges, dressed in uniforms, saluting the flag, and offering tons of advice. Over and over again, my mom had told me to avoid them since they would ask me a lot of questions and try to get me to tell them about her drug use. She told me with careful certainty that they would try to break up our family and take her away from me. The whole time they were at school that day, my heart pounded in fear. I tried to put my head down and closed my eyes hoping I wouldn't be seen.

They were there to talk about drug abuse and drug addiction. They led the classroom kids in shouts, their hands raised, yelling as if they were at a football game or a stadium event. It was frightening. I knew I had to hold onto my secret; I had to protect my family. They handed out pamphlets that talked about scientific studies and proven facts about drugs. They told us that using cocaine once can get you addicted. They talked about marijuana, LSD, mushrooms, and heroin with PCP. We got a whole education about street drugs. Then they said some things that twisted into my mind, wrapped around my heart and destroyed me.

After the yelling quieted down, one officer started talking in hushed tones. He looked around the room and told us that if we had one drug-addicted parent, then we were 50% more likely to become drug addicts ourselves. My small hands got sweaty and a sinking feeling grew in my stomach as I struggled with what he was saying. I started to do the math. Seemed like, since both of my parents were drug addicts, then of course 50% plus 50% equals 100%. Calculation complete. Destiny sealed. While the world around me had asked me over and over again what I was going to be when I grew up, someone was now telling me that my future had already been decided. I was a drug addict. That day, the one place I held out to be different, safe, and gentle—the hope for my future—was gone for me. Shattered in a school classroom presentation.

As the reality of their story seeped into my consciousness, a sense of captivity took over anything else that was in my heart, as if a fisherman's net had fallen over me and my fate was sealed. I accepted their prediction in my mind. *I, too, am a drug addict*, I thought.

I hadn't ever used drugs, yet. Throughout school, I had been so afraid of drugs and alcohol that even when the kids around me were getting high—some as young as me in the fourth or fifth grade—I had never tried anything. I even remember stealing weed from my mom in Portland and giving it to the neighborhood kids to fit in. As far as smoking it, I didn't go near any of it. It wasn't until four years later, when I was in the eighth grade, when I drank my first beer and experimented with pot, that Pandora's box was finally cracked open and the lies they told me were released and anchored into my life.

***

For me, the years of fearing that either I would follow in my dad's footsteps—drug addicted with thousands of track marks all over his body—or that I would just be another version of my mom—coming and going in and out of prison and psychiatric hospitals—finally came to a showdown. Strangely enough, since I didn't find myself turning into a drug addict overnight, I started to think that maybe I had won the battle. Maybe, I had somehow dodged the genetic flaw. After all, I felt in control. I saw myself as being like all the other kids who could hang with their alcohol and chill. I felt that I must have somehow freed myself from the future that D.A.R.E. had seen for me, and I started to believe that I could laugh at their certainty at my predictable future.

Turns out I was kidding myself. From the ages of 13 to 21, I was ticketed 15 times for consumption of alcohol as a minor. I stole merchandise and sold marijuana. I wasn't as free as I had thought.

The first time I got arrested, I was at a high school party in Peoria drinking with my friends. At this party there was a whole buffet of the scene of the mixed-up world of Peoria AZ in the 90's There were party crews looking to have a good time the Cowboys dressed in tight jeans and wearing cowboy hats. The Bros, the jock guys that usually ended up drinking too much and then there were the mafia guys, the drug dealers from Mexico- always easy to spot because they all had a uniform. It's funny when you think of mafia guys you usually picture slick back hair and suits well the mafia from Mexico had a different look. These guys all looked like well-paid cowboys, they wore big gold or silver belt buckles, cowboy boots, and white straw hats. These were the guys I always wanted to make friends with because knowing them meant you had a good connection back then. They were not as ruthless as they are now back then these guys were mostly simply famers just good old Mexican pot dealers.

Most of us were carrying guns. Since there were frequent outbreaks of violence in our neighborhood, we felt justified having guns of our own. Our high school parties always seemed to end with a shooting, stabbing, or with someone getting jumped. I've known too many people who'd go somewhere expecting a good time only to end up on the wrong end of a stray bullet, a knife or some other form of violence. Out of the eight people I knew at the party that night, two would die from firearms.

As the night got late, five or six guys started fighting with each other and it wasn't long before someone started shooting. I knew that a shakedown was imminent, so I told my friends to hide their guns. The cops would come, search everyone, and arrest the unlucky ones. Our attitude was that when a couple hundred people are partying and you're the one to get arrested, then you're the one taking the hit for the whole crew. The police couldn't fit everyone into the back of a squad car, so someone had to be sacrificed. That night, I was the sacrificial lamb.

The way the Peoria police did things back then was a joke. A bunch of police cars would plant themselves in front of a house, a helicopter would fly overhead, and a couple of cops would take their time searching people who smelled like alcohol. At the same time, hundreds of people would be doing their best to leave the party as quickly as they could. We knew we had only a couple of options: run, hide, or escape. If you were caught, you could get a ticket for drinking as a minor and be sent home. Or you could be arrested.

I had escaped many times and I had gotten stopped and ticketed many times and been let go. But this time was different. It was not my lucky night.

A helicopter with a spotlight crawled around the sky and the police on the ground blocked off the street. My friends and I were hiding our guns in the backyard of our friend's home when we heard the cops on loudspeakers yelling at us.

Do not move! Stay put!

Of course, the streets started to fill with the people leaving the party. The police knew what was going on and they knew that in that crowd of hundreds of people fleeing the scene there were young angry teenage boys like me and my crew.

The bright spotlight of the helicopter—we called it the *Ghetto Bird*—kept locking onto me. In a minute, we were all on the ground in front of the house, handcuffed. It was about 1 a.m. and the police decided to make an example of us and hauled a few of us off to jail.

I sat in the back of the police car with my head down, thinking that I was going to be kicked out of my grandparents' house. My dad was living in a truck camper in their backyard, boosting and getting high. It had been easy for me to get him to sign a ticket when I needed it, but now I was busted and I'd have to face my grandparents. I'd have to call them. My heart raced with fear. I'd heard of people getting arrested and getting killed by the police. I'd heard of inmate rape. I was 16 years old and drunk, but still I tried to talk my way out of the cuffs. At the precinct, I was told that if my grandparents came and got me, they would release me to their custody. If not, I would be taken to jail. I called my grandparents, not knowing if they'd come and get me or not. But they did come. Once in the car, I got the usual questions: *Do you want to grow up like your mom and dad? Are you going to waste your life, too?*

Within the hallways of my mind, the voice of the D.A.R.E. cop reverberated, fortified by my family's questions. These were the first steps in my downward decent into addiction. I didn't know it at the time, but it was the perfect storm. The unresolved pain of my childhood; the constant fear I was living in; the pressures of home life; watching my dad in heroin nods; the culture of the Barrio; the gangs.

All of these were becoming the building blocks of my self-identity. They were scattered around me, offering themselves up to me, and I was the chief mason adding to the walls of my own isolation, fed by the many influences of becoming a man.

Something died in me that night and it felt strangely good. My enduring fear of being arrested was finally vanquished and I began to feel free and victorious. Not for doing anything good, or for getting arrested, but for breaking through an ever-present fear. For me, it was a great feeling of accomplishment. The power that the police wields over people who grow up as I did is a different kind of power than the rest of society understands in the comfort of their social norms. The violence that just one cop can generate is rarely seen or appreciated in polite society. Yet, when you grow up around frustrated police who are burdened with arrest quotas and the many pressures of politics, who occasionally are even trying to make a difference, an energy builds that must be released—and it usually ends up in the streets. Fears of that palpable, explosive violence had haunted me for years; it had justified more and more of my involvement with drugs and alcohol. Being able to release it out of my system was huge.

With all my cries for help—the years of getting tickets, showing up for a court-ordered alcohol diversion class, and finding out where there was a place to drink and get high—you would think that our land of the free and home of the brave would respond with some solutions and help instead of constant punitive resolve. It didn't. There was one person who briefly helped lift me out of my destiny—it just wasn't enough.

When I was in the tenth grade, the courts finally sent me to see a counselor. During the summer, just before school started up again, my crew and I had stolen about 97 bottles of hard alcohol from four stores in town. I started to get a little cocky and careless with all my conquests. One fall school day, during lunch break, I got caught shoplifting a pack of Marlboro 25 cigarettes and a bottle of whiskey on a dare. (More irony, right?) It was pretty embarrassing because all the kids from school where in the parking lot eating lunch when the cops put me in the back of their cruiser as an example to the others. Of course, my grandparents had to come and get me out of custody since I was still a minor, so my shame grew worse.

During the court proceedings, I was assigned a counselor. My grandfather and I went to see him together. The guy was nice enough, so I guess I opened up about my childhood and told him about what I had been through. The counselor looked at my grandpa and said, *Sir, I see young people like your grandson all the time, and I can tell you that he is not as bad as most of the others.* He said, *When they've grown up like he has, I usually end up seeing them for murder or rape or burglary. Most of the kids I see with this kind of background are not here for shoplifting. You're one of the lucky ones. I think your grandson is going to be okay.*

Crazy as it sounds, with that one counselor's okay, I felt that I had everything all under control again. It was the first time I can remember that person in authority looked at my past and told me I was going to be okay. It was the first time that felt like I was not as bad as I had told myself I was. The state signed off on me because I talked my way out of the counseling sessions. Unfortunately, I was still under the spell that was cast over me when I first became a drug addict way back in Sunnyside elementary school in Portland Oregon when the D.A.R.E. cops told me that's all I'd ever be.

Since that day in class with the D.A.R.E. officers, I had been living up to their prediction and fulfilling their prophecy. That place of self-identity would create such a gravity within me that my whole life would be absorbed into its energy. From my early years of drinking and smoking pot, to using heroin with my dad, to smoking crack, stealing, and getting locked up as an adult in county jail, my life continued to unravel. Eventually, getting sent to state and federal prison, it was all a part of the design of my self-identity, which I thought I had no say in. But I did.

It was not until many years later, in a prison yard in Arizona, that I would begin to realize that my parents' war with their adopted culture was a war that would not be won by fighting it. I knew that I had to try to make a change and I had to make a difference in my life. By that time, I was the father of a beautiful young girl and I wanted to try to change for her and for myself.

I was also sick of living the lifestyle I had inherited. I was tired. Tired of the self-destructive behavior that was robbing me of choices. Tired of feeling that I could die at any moment. Tired of being afraid of the police. Tired of being afraid at all. I was fed up with owing people money and keeping track of the people who owed me money. I was just done.

Ironically, prison ended up contributing to my self-empowerment, as it helped me let go of my fear of the police. Being around the guards all day and getting to know them somehow helped destroy the ideas that the police were less than human and capable of destroying my life. It was an empowering breakthrough for me. Yet, I couldn't shake the questions I had about what got me in my inner prison in the first place. *Why doesn't our culture or our communities help people come back to society by addressing their issues? Why are mental illnesses in children ignored so often? Why isn't trauma recognized for what it is—a debilitating seed that germinates into survival tactics that hurt the host as much as the enemy?* Our culture's usual responses to the needs of the drug-addicted, the children, and others who have only minimal resources are in so many ways more hurtful than helpful to the now millions of generational people like me living with these inherited traumas.

***

By sharing with you the unfolding of my suffering, I'm hoping you'll see that I found the greatest gifts I have to give right within the pain that I endured. With the help of *The Sacred 7*, I finally understood that this is my medicine. I learned that, whether it's in the form of iron bars and cold glass, addictive behaviors, or self-chastising and destructive thinking, everyone lives in some sort of captivity. At the same time, I discovered that we all can access the ability to cultivate our unique medicine to bring about personal and community transformation. We can free ourselves from what binds us to the victim mentality and to the conviction of separation in our hearts.

The spiritual practice gifted by *The Sacred 7* gives us new choices about what to do with our emotions and reactions to what life throws at us. It absorbs and neutralizes the sensationalism of the news media and the politically ambitious. It allows the banter and fear stoked by social media and even those in your community to be seen for who and what they are. Most importantly, it provides a pathway of transformation that embraces the truth of your life and the truth of who you are so that you can experience a sense of sovereignty that cannot be determined, defined, or destroyed by anyone or anything. Within prison walls, I found the deepest of freedoms and discovered the seeds of a spiritual path that is both ancient in origin yet applicable to a contemporary lifestyle. It is an open-hearted process that can free us from the bindings of limiting emotions, open us up to a transcendent state of consciousness and enable us to live optimal and abundant lives.

CHAPTER 4

AWAKENING

In our contemporary culture, most of us are taught from an early age that who we are is what we do. We are asked again and again what we want to be when we grow up—as if we're not enough already—and the answer to the question is always a job title. Firefighter. Mother. Space engineer. Doctor. Rockstar. And whether we stick to these titles or take on other ones that are pushed upon us, we weave a story that attaches itself to our consciousness and locks us into a self-limiting relationship until the last breath we breathe.

These stories are what I call the I AM statements that we tell ourselves over and over again and associate ourselves in that identity. Yet, they end up limiting our human experience and creating a realm of captivity within which we can't help but struggle. What are the containers we limit ourselves to? I AM a business owner. I AM a carpenter. I AM a musician. I AM an addict. But what do these definitions mean to your soul? What does it mean to your relationship with the air, the water, the fire, and to the earth? More importantly, how is it limiting your relationship with yourself?

There was a time in European history when the people of the land were forced to come into the castle of the lords and nobles and present themselves. Perhaps, it was the fear of tribal hordes and promise of protection or to avoid slavery, or perhaps to fulfill it, as they acknowledged the authority of those in power, they were forced to give up their ancestry, the stories of their lineage, and often their connection to the lands they came from. As the nobility moved to control them, they changed their names—and identities—to Smiths, Carpenters, Tailors, Stewards, Knights, Parsons, and Singers—names that reflected their laboring and service to the nobility. They were their jobs, stripped of connection to their history, their family, and the earth. More, they were disconnected from a system of self-identity that gave them meaning, purpose, connection, and spiritual freedom.

The destruction of self-identity has occurred in every culture, taken place among every people, and been forced upon peoples across every land. The clan identity, the connection to lands of their own ancestors, and the fires of ancient ceremonies have at some point been taken from the ancestors of all the Smiths and Carpenters of the world by the sword. Still today, the tradition continues. Prisons and military tactics are the contemporary tools that keep people of different cultures isolated and disconnected. Fear tactics, "education," law, and religions are now the tools of assimilation, and if they don't work, then guns and prison will do.

AWAKENING

Without the kind of elemental connection to the earth that The Sacred 7, it is easy to break up families, bomb communities, and oppress people. The void of captivity defined by the lack of a connected self-identity has led to historic rates of suicide, overdose, drug addiction, and incarceration.

The Sacred 7 offers a pathway back to freedom and sovereignty by helping us untangle the concepts of self-identity that we have created and that been imposed upon us. This ancient technology offers a new path to understanding the mystery of the I AM.

I have known myself as an addict, a felon, a criminal, an entrepreneur, a Christian, an Apache, a White Man, A Mexican, a Chicano, a father, a son, a boyfriend, a husband, a warrior, a peacemaker, a gangster, a student, a saint, a prophet, a healer, an athlete, a preacher, a Buddhist, a yogi, and a loser... and many more. These have been my I AM's: representing who I understood myself to be at one point or another. While it's comforting to have a label to call ourselves, the confusion, suffering, and disconnection engendered by disparate and conflicting titles like these are greater than we realize.

The illusions of I AM statements can be dangerous. These thoughts are building blocks that both form a foundation and build a structure of identity. And before we know it, we are contained in the illusion we unwittingly built. We become an actor in our own story. What's more, it's usually a story that is dictated by someone else's concept of who we are. The illusory I AM story is a state of captivity that robs us of many choices we'd otherwise make. We override the feelings within our own souls, and we begin to justify our feelings and experiences by the outside influences that are keeping us captive. We are taken into a kind of enslavement to other people's social and even cultural ideologies. These societal social structures encourage us to establish these ideas about ourselves that are then fortified within the metaphysical architectural fields of energy.

My I AM statements led me right to prison. As a child of two junkies and a person with brown skin, I had been convinced of many things about myself, fed by characters on television, by the words of the D.A.R.E. officers and others in authority, and sometimes by those people closest to me. I became captivated within that energetic framework; that captivity led to behaviors, and those behaviors eventually manifested as iron bars.

Self-inflicted incarceration is not limited to the contemporary world of punitive justice, mass incarceration, and prisons for profit. Sometimes, it can be in family or cultural stereotypes. Today these cultural and family stereotypes form just as dense of a metaphysical architecture of captivity as some of the stereotypes that I have had to overcome, although they are not necessarily seen in the same way. For instance, I have heard countless interviews with artists and entrepreneurs from a variety of backgrounds say something to the effect of, My family were immigrants, and everyone wanted me to be doctor. Or, Everyone in my family was an engineer. Since I am from such-and-such ethnic group, I am supposed to be an engineer.

These types of collective agreements create an energetic architecture of thought, even prayer, for an individual to live in a purpose driven existence. For many people the comfort of this "plan" is too easy to refuse and they fall into the flow of a state of imprisonment, giving up their personal calling to pursue nothing more than a stereotype.

AWAKENING

I believe this is why so many professions are comprised largely of only one ethnic group of people. The community and family of those individuals have decided to hold that metaphysical architecture.

Limitations are inflicted on people within all of the cultures that have slowly but surely placed their faith in identifying people as jobs. Along with the industrialization of most of the cultures around the world came the destruction of the peoples' connection to the basic elements—air, water, fire, earth, gravity, time, and spirit —and to the lands of their ancestors, confining people into predictable and reasonable walks of life.

What then grew within that fertile void was a psychological cycle of needing to be more, have more, and do more. The search for the answer to What am I going to be when I grow up? went viral, fueling belief in not being enough and not having enough, causing tremendous suffering and even self-inflicted harm.

It wasn't until I was incarcerated in an Arizona state prison that I started to learn how to be free. The ironic thing was, I was there by "mistake". I had a federal detainer at the time, which meant, according to the guidelines of the federal prison system, that I should be placed in a medium-security facility, or worse. But because of the slip-up, I found myself at Fort Grant State Prison in Safford, Arizona, a minimum-security facility where it just so happened that members of both sides of my own family had spent time. For a moment, I thought my federal charges of conspiracy with the intent to distribute LSD and psilocybin mushrooms had been dropped. Later, I found out it was just the Hand of Providence guiding me to a place in which I could see in dramatic fashion the path of my family and how it was time for me to make a change.

Andrew Wayne, Thomas Ecker

It was an awakening moment for me. I was confronted with memories of visiting my father on that same prison yard as a child, the smell of the visiting room, the fear. I would cycle through the memories, flashing back to my childhood, and feeling the collective reinforcement that I would someday follow the same path. Like a self-fulling prophecy, I had already seen myself behind the razor wire fence and guard tower positioned against the back drop of the beautiful wide-open desert of Arizona.

They were not just contemporary walls built for the newest form of American warfare—the war on drugs. No, they were the walls that have broken free men for years. The walls of Fort Grant had held my maternal ancestors, the prison was famously part of the Apache wars and was rumored to hold the defiant Chiricahua Apache warrior, powerful medicine man, and leader of the Bedonkohe Clan Goyahkla, known to the world as Geronimo. Even my powerful Apache ancestors, who fought for freedom, died in captivity. It would take this deliberate unfolding of the story of conflict for me to walk away from a path that had been laid down by the outlaws and freedom fighters of generations.

I was in an environment that was made for me: my father, my ancestors, my neighborhood, and even my own past had walked the walls of that prison.

It was fate that put me there, a perfect alignment of forces out of the control of the government ordinances of incarceration or anything other than Providence. And it launched my journey to the freedom of self-discovery, liberation, and ultimately, sovereignty, that I had sought for so long. It felt like I'd been given a clear sign from the Creator that I was being handed an opportunity to change my direction and my fortune.

AWAKENING

The culture of prison life at Fort Grant was eerily comfortable to me. It was too familiar; it was an energy that I knew instinctively; it was a part of me. I clearly understood virtually every aspect of it: the captivity, the smell, the vibration, the written and unwritten rules, and the culture. In a lot of ways, I saw myself as being bred to survive it. Set in motion by the words of the D.A.R.E. officers amid the chaotic climate of a drug-addicted, criminal lifestyle, I found myself easily identifying with a world that many considered to be the worst of the worst, the end of the line, the lowest of the low.

Once again, the forces of the Universe called for more change in my life. Soon after my awakening at Fort Grant, prison authorities realized their mistake and decided to send me to a medium-security facility located at the base of the sacred mountain of my Apache ancestors, known today as Mount Graham. Meanwhile, pending the transfer, they put me into restrictive housing, which meant 23 hours of lockdown per day, no movement, and no visits. I was in confinement for almost a month while the system tried to figure out what to do with me. It was the beginning of a period of isolation that actually served me. If I had remained around those who knew my family history of crime and drugs, then the familiar voices of my neighborhood, my friends, and the established criminal identity of my family at Fort Grant might have distracted me from the depth of what was about to happen within me.

A hope arose in the unlikeliest of ways. Just as I was in the process of getting moved to Mount Graham, a courage rose up in me to find out the truth about something that had been haunting me.

When I first started doing heroin, it really pained my dad. It was what he did about it surprised me—he got me high.

The first time it happened, we sat in the car of his crime partner, a guy we used to call Big Nose Chris, a guy my dad met at Fort Grant. Later, they hooked up on the streets and boosted together for years. For a while, we'd only use just after a boost when we would steal together. I'd help him out by being a decoy in the stores, to draw the security off of him, or by driving. For years, I thought there was a real likelihood that he not only turned me on to a really good heroin connection but also that he had passed on his Hepatitis C. In other words, it was possible that I had not only taken on his drug habit and criminal lifestyle but also the disease that eventually took his life. That thought fed my habit of not really caring about my life. It was always in the back of my mind whenever I did a crime or did drugs, and in many ways, it fueled my darker actions.

Now, you would think that because almost 80% of people with a history of intravenous drug use have Hep C that the prison system would make it mandatory to test for it. They do not. While I was at Fort Grant, I wrestled with the idea of getting tested until I decided to just do it. Then, when I was literally in the holding cell, waiting for the bus to take me to the other prison, I thought about how easy it is for paperwork of transferred prisoners to get lost in the shuffle. I realized that if I wanted to know the truth, I had to act right away. So, I asked a detention officer if he could find out my test results for me. I told him I needed to know the truth and I didn't want to pass something on to someone else unknowingly. He was a kind man. I had worked for him on the yard before, we locked eyes from behind the metal fence, he told me he would call to the medical center for the results.

His desk was just across from me in the holding room. I sat there as he picked up the phone and watched everything as if it was in slow motion. After what seemed like forever, he looked over at me and told me that no one was answering. My heart sank and thought I would have to get up the courage again at the next prison to find out if I was being handed a life sentence, since that was before the new treatments were available, and the disease was considered terminal. The officer looked over at me once again, asking me if I thought I had it. I told him I did. My dad died of Hep C, and we used to do heroin together, I explained. He looked at the ground as if someone had taken the air right out of his sails. I'll just go down there, he said.

I sat there alone in that tiny steel cage made of chain link fence with a million thoughts going through my mind. I found the courage to say a prayer. Then he walked in and told me the test results were back. I was negative for Hep C. I had not gotten the virus.

For a moment, I felt something of an energetic transfer of captivity that I would later think of as a shift in the metaphysical architecture of identity. My mind had let go of my death sentence. As I sat in awe of God and my life in that tiny fenced-in room and felt into the experience, I felt waves of bliss flowing through me as the years of conditioning began to fade into the truth of what I thought was a miracle.

It was as if a window to my soul had opened and I felt the Hand of God drawing a map that led me from the foothills of sorrow into the arms of comfort. Once again, I felt that the Grand Design was there within the realm of possibility; I only needed to walk out into the field of its energy.

I remained at Mount Graham for only a couple of months before being sent to a maximum-security facility in the prison city of Florence, Arizona; there I was held for eighteen months. Florence was, and still is, literally a city of prisons and prison workers. Of all places, it was there that my journey to discovering The Sacred 7 and my own sovereignty would begin. Ironically, it began the same way my captivity had begun: with the energetic displacement and manifestation of self-identity.

I was being held at a Corrections Corporation of America (CCA), more recently rebranded as CoreCivic, a corporate prison for hire. These for-profit prisons have been a solution to the mass incarceration and criminalization of immigration that our country's political climate has produced. When I arrived there, the population was 80% illegal immigrants, mostly Mexican nationals, and some from Central America. They were held without a release date or the ability to bond. They were federal detainees, held without any rights, most of them farmers and construction workers. Some were fleeing the gangs and crimes in their home countries and got caught at the border.

The prison population was a mix of people from many walks of life. There were countless men who, although raised in the U.S., were getting deported to their countries of birth. Many had no friends or family there and no knowledge of the culture. Some did not even know how to speak fluent Spanish, but none of that mattered. I met one man whose parents had gone to Mexico when his mother was pregnant with him because they were afraid that the Vietnam war would cause him to be drafted. Besides that, he was all American. The stories were all too common: poor people getting locked up for political or financial profit. There were also major drug dealers, but they were not your average crack or cocaine dealers on the street. These were guys running pounds of weight for the cartels.

AWAKENING

Most of them were business people, not stereotypical gang members that you see in the fear-filled news media. There was also a population of Native Americans since the federal government serves the reservations and the Bureau of Indian Affairs sends their offenders to federal prison, too.

One of the strange things about being at CCA was that it didn't seem to matter what you were in for. Everyone was all mixed in together. In most detention institutions, inmates are separated based on the type of crime they were charged with or how much of a threat to society they seemed to be. Not at CCA, I served time alongside people who had committed all degrees of crimes, from mail fraud to multiple murders. I felt more alone than ever. Since my name and reputation were well known in the criminal world of Arizona, I had friends in almost every jail I had ever been in. But CCA was different. I hardly knew anyone.

One day, as I sat in a small concrete room with my door partially closed to help drown out the sounds of 200 prisoners in the unit, I felt a questioning of Who am I? What am I? begin to swirl in my stomach. It was as if a highly energetic child was swimming around in the base of my abdomen. I was pondering my life, my situation, and my sentence, and I was asking myself Why.

I was being charged with criminal conspiracy with intent to distribute LSD and psilocybin mushrooms. The plea deal was offering me 10 years to life. The I AM inside me was crushed under the massive weight of this possibility. Whatever power my mind had to control the situation was gone; I was left with nothing to bear the burden of my life choices. There was no more room for blaming my life as a child; no more room for saying it was the drugs that made me do it—all that was gone. I was simply swimming in the depths of the tragedy of my life.

I resurfaced from my deep reflection and decided I wasn't going to be just another captive to the system, to myself, to my family, to my neighborhood—to anything. I wasn't going to follow in the footsteps of my mother and father and become just one more self-fulfilling prophecy. I was going to change, even if it meant being a monk for 25 years. When I got out, I wanted to do something better.

It became clear to me that there was no more need to fight the destructive battle of internal demise that had been fueled by the culture of my childhood. Instead, I became filled with refreshing thoughts of being free. I started to feel a new life began to bud inside of me that would lead me to a new world of infinite possibilities.

My thoughts began to build a new metaphysical architecture for my life out of the rubble of the crushed I AM's that had developed over the years. A spacious sense of openness began to bud within me and guide me. As I traveled on this new road, I felt a sense of flow that seemed to manifest the tools I needed to build a place of my own design—the design of freedom.

The I AM that my long-standing dwelling place had created was comfortable. It was seasoned and well maintained, and it would take courage to let go of. My new path was built only by hope and faith; the certainties of survival were unclear; the road was being laid down as walked. In the midst of generational incarceration, I jumped into a sea of uncertain outcomes like a traveler destined for a new place. I found the courage to leave what had become my resident state of mental slavery. It had been generations in the making, so I needed to clear a new path within myself and for myself. I had to find my

AWAKENING

own freedom from drug culture—not just freedom from using, but freedom from the lifestyle— in order to get a foothold on the path of sovereignty.

It was time for a change.

I had never been much of reader; my life had never felt safe enough to open the doorway that reading provides. The desecration brought on by addiction and dysfunction around me led me to find a way to explore new worlds and ideas in books.

Those new ideas would come from a person I trusted. The only person I knew from the outside was someone who was being held on the same charges as me. We called him Foot Bear. He was a very spiritual person and was as close to being free as anyone I had ever met. We stood out in the prison population like sore thumbs, looking like a couple of guys who had just walked out of the woods. I had dreadlocks down my back, and his almost touched the floor.

Foot Bear had been my connection and partner in an LSD/ mushroom and high-quality marijuana business. We had sold a lot of LSD together—so much that I was known everywhere I went. Even in the grocery store, someone would inevitably walk up to me and tell me they knew someone that did business with a dealer I knew. Foot Bear was the connection and I was the soldier working the concerts, raves, and streets. We made a lot of money in those days, even though that wasn't really my motivation.

The constructs of the I AM statements of my life had created me as a drug a dealer. I remember fortifying those ideas in my mind when thousands of dollars would be in a deal, and everyone was feeling edgy. The look of fear in the eyes of everyone doing the exchange comforted me as I judged their fear as weakness. I would tell myself, You grew up in this. You were made for these moments. I had earned that mental strength from years of surviving the lifestyle, and I was comfortable when others were on edge and in fear.

When I sold LSD, I felt like I sold a ticket out of the system. For me, LSD and mushrooms were like arrows that pierced the heart of violence and caused painted-faced people of every color to play drums and dance together. They were a weapon, a chemical stone in the sling of my hand as I stood like David facing my personal Goliath. To me, that Goliath had beaten my mother, destroyed my father, and willed me in and out of jail. It had put me in a mental prison, created by the structure of the nation's culture. My Goliath was the system of the United States Government.

By some miracle, both Foot Bear and I were able to get our 10-year sentence reduced to three. It was a miracle to me because if I had been caught with anyone else, my life would have taken a very different turn. Neither one of us even being asked to testify against anyone or become informants.

Foot Bear also gave me the keys to another trip that would last longer than any of the others we had experienced together. He introduced me to the first book on my spiritual journey, which I would read from beginning to end: Bo Lozoff's book, 'We're All Doing Time'. The book was (and is still) donated for free to prisoners around the world by The Prison Ashram Project. When the book arrived in the mail for me, it felt like a lifeline to the outside world, beyond the walls, smells, barbed wire, violence, and isolation of prison life. As I read it, my eyes began to open to what was really keeping me incarcerated in my life.

AWAKENING

I had never read anything like it before. In its pages—filled with spiritual stories from the Christian saints to yoga and meditation practices—I started to understand that captivity is a spiritual condition—and to overcome a spiritual condition, you have to practice spirituality. What a revelation!

I began to recognize that spirituality was even reflected within the walls of my experiences in prison. For example, prison talk is filled with the stories of the street; the exploits of criminal life are a part of almost every conversation. The prison classrooms are the "yard," wherever we work out, or maybe the game room where we play chess, cards, or board games. They are filled with some of the filthiest language you can imagine. Everything from cussing to the vulgar exploits of women. The class topic could easily have been "How to be a Better Criminal."

With the help of the wisdom within the book I was reading, I started to see certain things in a new light. I noticed that when the "spiritual" men in the prison—sometimes Christian, sometime Islamic—entered a room, the climate would change. In their presence, the tough gangster talk would calm down; some of the gangsters even stuttered a little.

Gabriel was from Mexico. He was known for fasting sometimes 40-50 days on nothing but water, juice, and milk. Sammy, from Nigeria, had such a presence that I saw groups of people break off as he walked through the prison—not by saying anything, just by being. I thought: These guys have real power. I began to learn that spirituality is not about overcoming but about transcending and transforming a situation. It's not about being a criminal; it's about being a child of God. It's about finding the I AM statements that serve your highest self, your medicine, and that bring you power into your life.

My yearning for freedom from captivity and my discovery of spirituality led me to religion. In prison, Christianity was my only choice; they sure weren't offering any yoga or Tai Chi or Buddhist meditation. So I dove into Christianity full-on, learning about service and loving God. I helped out in a ministry that was established by the prison Church Fellowship. We'd buy extra shower shoes and soap so the ministry could give guys just coming onto the yard a small bag filled with shower shoes, soap, and even a candy bar. I had many amazing life-changing experiences while serving God in prison for the three years I was there.

I was incredibly hungry for God. I read the Bible, fasted, prayed deeply, and participated in everything I could. The religious life was challenging at times, but it felt a lot easier than dealing with the struggles of my old way of thinking. It gave me a lot to feast on as it brought many powerful teachings into my life that have stayed with me and been a comfort in my times of need.

As I practiced my spirituality in prison, the power to manipulate reality seemed to unfold before my eyes. My influence grew, and it felt as if I was finding a path. I discovered that leaving one state of self-identity and finding another—what some call cognitive dissonance—is the state in which transformation is still uncertain. When I began to feel the emergence of a new life of freedom from the captivity of my destructive self-identity, the universe began to reveal the plan. As I started to share it with others, the manifestation of that abundance became clear in new and meaningful relationships.

I had a lot of time to focus on myself, and I started to share my new-found love of spirituality as my process

AWAKENING

unfolded. I began to write letters to the many people who were involved in my criminal and drug-addicted life, telling of the power of God's love. One day, a friend that who was still actively using heroin left one of my letters on his kitchen counter and his mom happened to pick it up and read it. She later told me that the words on the paper felt inspired by God and she felt compelled to help me. Her name was Kathy, and she became a friend and advocate. Until then, no one on the outside had cared enough to visit me, but Kathy would. She put money on my books, sent me cards on my birthday and holidays, and even once picked up an old friend to come and see me. It was the first of what would turn into many signs that encouraged me to stay on the path of self-realization and spirituality.

***

When my three years were up, and I was released from prison, I started doing missionary work with children in low-income communities and kids with drug-addicted or incarcerated parents. I founded and served as a pastor at The Redemption House, which provided transitional living spaces for men and women coming out of prison and off the streets. It was a safe place for people to learn about God, pray, and be around others struggling with addiction.

At one point, we had over nine houses filled with men and women needing help. I named the ministry Redemption House because redemption was a theme of mine while in prison. For me, redemption meant to be bought back from slavery, to become free and sovereign. Redemption has meant a lot to me, so much so that while in prison I had the word tattooed on my back as a timeless reminder of the freedom that spirituality has given me.

For five years, I fell deeply into the evangelical world, answering what I thought was my calling. But then the blinders of my zealous desire to serve began to dissolve, and I began to see more of the truth of the evangelical world. I started to notice the judgements, the elitism, and the separation in the men's breakfasts, the church outings, and Christian business groups I was attending. Politics and agenda had superseded the purpose of the teachings of Christ with a focus on conquering the world of "sinners." My relationship with a community that had given me so much was being questioned, and my heart didn't feel that it had anything to do with my relationship with God. In fact, my relationship with the Source had begun to broaden and become more expansive. I began to experience a profound Presence that is a lot more fluid, pliable, available, and yet more mysterious than ever before.

The religious path I had been following had offered me some of the safety and comfort I had craved for a long time. It was easy at first to follow the lead of church leaders and to finally have answers to some of the most perplexing questions I had about my life. Questions like: Why had so many people in my life, purposely or not, hurt, abused, or neglected me as child? I was comforted with the simple idea that it was because "they didn't know Jesus," and that mollified me for a while. Still, deep inside me, it didn't feel right. Something felt wrong about some of us being considered God's chosen people since it implied an uneven playing field even where God was concerned. It caused me to start questioning my beliefs around the entire Christian worldview.

Unfortunately, within Christianity, like most structured religions around the world, there is a certain spirit of separation that underlies its precepts. It's a voice that causes us to say that maybe we're better than someone else, or maybe our ideology is better than someone else's. Maybe it claims that we're going to go to some utopian place because of our ideology. Inside that idea of separation, our metaphysical architecture creates a container of safety within our own idea of who we are. At the same time, inside of that seeming safety, there is a certain obligation to let go of one's truest self. So many of us end up completely compromising our integrity along with the love that dwells inside of us that is there to be expressed.

Then, I experienced something that gave me insight into the captivity of religion and the nature of true freedom. It would change the course of my spiritual awakening.

I had been hired under a substance abuse and mental health services grant to go and share the drum with the children and elders of the Havasupai Nation at the bottom of the Grand Canyon. The intent was to help reduce the incidence of suicide there. The Havasupai are the most remote Native American tribe in the continental United States. Only about 700 of them live down in the Canyon and the only way anyone can get there is by horseback, by foot, or by helicopter; they have no roads, no airstrips, and no train tracks that lead into the village. Being so isolated, you'd think that they'd be protected from the dangerous and destructive forces of drugs, alcohol, and thoughts of suicide, but the struggle for survival is very real even in the midst of one of the most beautiful places on the planet.

By that time, I had facilitated thousands of transformative drum circles, yet I felt an uncertainty emerge in me about working with the Havasupai. The magnitude of working with the most remote native American tribe in the continental United States was overwhelming. As I stood at what the people in the village of Supai call Hilltop— the loading area for the helicopter that brings people, food, and materials to the village all day long, I felt myself to be at some sort of threshold. Hilltop is the last gateway to the world; from there, a traveler descends into the canyon and travels to the small village of around 700 people. It is the only connection to modern transportation, and it provides the only access to the road from the village. Overlooking the layers of the red, pink, grey, and black rock of the beautiful Grand Canyon, I was confronted with myself, and I sank into the pain of not being born of the right family, having the right education, being the right anything. At that point in my life, I been clean from drugs for about ten years, had worked hard on myself, had created ministries and had helped so many people. Yet there I was—still— the son of two junkies, inserted into an ancient tribe that had survived the changing of countries, conquerors, and countless attempts by outside forces to destroy their ways of life. They had stood strong defying cultural assimilation. One of the tribal elders, a blind singer and holy man named Tiny, said it best: *"We are the Havasubaja (the traditional name of the Havasupai). We have lived in the bottom of the Grand Canyon for ten thousand years, and we are going to keep on living right here in the bottom of the Grand Canyon for another ten thousand years." In the midst of such ancestral power and wisdom, I found myself wondering, What could I possibly have to give that means anything?*

I knew that inner doubt well: I had experienced it many times before when I worked with people who were absorbed in overwhelming circumstances. I had felt it when I looked into the eyes of addicts and children in deep human crisis and saw myself reflected there. The doubt felt like an open space of questioning my ability and purpose. Yet, the questioning also seems to light my path to a perfect place of humility, where only an unprecedented reliance on something greater than myself shows up and performs the miracles I didn't even know I was asking for.

Then my inner voice—that which is connected to the vastness of self-understanding and to the universe itself—spoke loudly within me. *Talk to them about being a suicide survivor and the way your parents died*, it said. The power of The Sacred 7 began to take hold again, showing me that my true medicine was not just in my years of drumming or in leading transformative experiences but in the power that I was incarnated to share. My inner voice connected to Source, wanted nothing more than for me to be myself, to find my power, and show up. Moved by the signs of pain and suffering I saw in the people there, I let myself share my personal story. I shared with them about being so broken inside that the only way I could stop the pain was to cut myself. I shared with them the pain of watching most of the native side of my family die of drugs and alcohol. I told them what the drum meant to me, that it was a tool to connect to Spirit and express the hurt from the years of neglect and abuse. I realized later that I was using the medicine of my trauma to benefit the community. My vulnerability seemed to open up the group and shift the energy to allow more direct honesty about topics that weren't normally discussed.

It felt incredibly rewarding to me to sit in drum circles with the children of the village and share with them the power of drumming. It satisfied some deeper calling than I had ever known in the worlds of religion. I had no agenda to make people donate to a church or to win souls. I was only there to help people survive and to let them know they're not alone.

One day, in a drum circle with the youth of the village, I asked the group if someone would play on the drum the way they felt when they were bullied at school. Studies have shown a connection between bullying and suicide, so it was a big part of our mission to speak to that. One young Havasupai girl beat the drum so loudly and intensely that it felt like the walls of community center where going to fall in. I felt deeply connected to her in that moment; it was as if she was playing my song. Through her drumming, I felt my own inner self release the suffering of years of schoolyard bullying. Then, I invited the group to share what they felt when she played that. At first, it was a challenge to get any of the youth to speak. But once the ice was broken, a torrent was released. The kids shouted feeling words in a choir of release. For a moment that seemed infinite, the compressed, suppressed feelings of these children were opened as the ancient tool of the drum hammered against the density of the walls of energetic captivity and smashed through the resistance. All so a child could feel once again. In that brief moment, I felt our collective history was changed. There was not a person in the circle that day was not transformed by the experience.

Soon after that, my small crew and I accepted the *Elders'* invitation to their sweat lodge, a sacred purification ceremony, in our honor. The ceremony is meaningful to all when it is performed, and a lot of work is done to prepare for it. The wood must be chopped, the stones must be gathered, the water needs to be put in buckets, and offerings need to be made. We were brought to an earth hut made from the rich red dirt and branches of the trees of the canyon, which were molded into a womb-shaped room with only one door, covered by a blanket.

AWAKENING

The lodge sat next to a beautiful stream that flows from the depths of the canyon and that glows with a beautiful luminescent blue-green hue. This water is what defines the tribe, whose name, *Havasupai, means the people of the blue-green water.* We started by sitting around the fire. The singer, Roland, one of the last sons of the great *Havasupai Chiefs*, spoke about many things, including the origins of fire and the gratitude he had for us coming to share the drum and help his people.

Just as the ceremony was about to begin, a young girl and her mom came through the doorway of the hut. The woman spoke to Roland in the language of the Havasupai. Roland turned to the rest of us and told us that the little girl was his granddaughter and she wanted to come to the sweat lodge, so her mom brought her. I felt comforted by their innocence and presence in the lodge.

As stones began to sizzle and the sage and cedar were beginning to burn, I felt taken back to my origins of life. I prayed for myself and for the other people who were in our program. The gourd sounded like a bell ringing to quiet my mind chatter. A friend of mine and fellow Lipan Apache, Roman Orona, brought his drum and the Apache drum beat felt like the heartbeat of Mother Earth. The Havasupai songs in the air were literally thousands of years old and acted like a vibrational doorway to take me where I needed to go. I felt them piercing my consciousness and rewiring the broken parts of my mind. Every possible human emotion came to the surface—feelings of life, death, and everything in between—to purge something from within me and transform me. I was immersed in an ancient practice of rebirth. I had been to countless sweat lodges before, but this one took me far beyond where I had been.

The intensity and power of the experience left me wanting to confront my ideas of reality and my religious understandings of life. How could I reconcile the beauty and depth of these experiences with my Christian ideas? I didn't know how to process it and embrace both worlds in my heart and mind.

When I went to bed that evening, an image of a horrid, red-eyed, black figure loomed in my mind like a demon taunting me. As the image danced in front of my closed eyes, my heart started beating quickly, and my palms went into a sweat. Then I remembered an Asian shamanic practice for these kinds of situations. When confronted with demons, master shamans would say, I love you and You're beautiful to the spirit, over and over again. The practice acknowledges that what the energy really wants is to transcend its karma and work out its spiritual process, and the repetition helps it do that. I remembered the practice, used by these medicine men of faraway lands, and I began to realize that the monster I was dealing with was simply a part of me that was trying to reveal itself. I decided that I needed to love it and find its beauty, just as the shamanic practice suggests. So, I closed my eyes and repeated, *I love you. You are beautiful. I accept you. I'm not afraid.*

I spoke it. I chanted it. I whispered it. And after a period of looking within at that demonic being and loving that dark part of myself, I felt a transformation in my own heart. I got a deeper glimpse into who I was and who I am. Almost immediately, the horrible entity melted back into the darkness. I soon fell asleep and got the best rest of my life.

It was the first time in my life that I had ever experienced such a power inside myself. I was beginning to understand that I didn't need to rely on the outside force of a judgmental God or religion, but instead I could draw from an internal relationship that allows me to transform the world and to live a beautiful life. It was the beginning of a deeper relationship with God than I had known before and I was grateful.

After the sweat lodge, the revelations continued. I was able to learn more about myself through my connection to the stones, the water, the drum, the songs, and the prayers. I began to see the divides of separation, the religious confusion, and the truth of the mysteriousness of spirituality. As my perceived separation from people faded away, my sense of separation from the animals, the air, water, fire, earth, gravity, time, and *Spirit* faded as well. I discovered that everybody is whole. I saw deeper into myself in *Havasupai* than I ever had before.

For the record, I still love the teachings of Christ; they've really impacted my life. Jesus' mission was all about freedom. He said, *I've come to take the captivity captive.* But as I followed the teachings of Christ as I had been taught them, I began to bump into the brick walls of the religion's imposing limitations. Even when I had attended a beautiful guided imagery class a year or so before, I found myself afraid to go deeper into myself because I had been taught by my Christian teachers not to feel grief or sadness. God was supposed to be my Happy Drug. Anything else was not okay. That didn't feel right to me.

***

Real freedom came to me in 2012, when I sat in an ancestral hogan in Northern Arizona, along with 30 or so other seekers, and I first heard someone speak their identity through an ancient introduction. For me, it was a turning point: the many spiritual practices I had embarked on, the lifelong hurt, pain, and practice of trying to figure things out were bearing fruit. I felt a real power in those who introduced themselves, and I felt in my core that this authentic form of spirituality was what I needed—maybe what the world needed—to become free again.

The experience in *Hogan* made me hunger to learn more about who I was and who my ancestors were. I delved into learning more about my heritage, and I got my DNA tested. I started to think that being native meant more than being some savage thief like the Hollywood westerns depicted us.

And I started practicing the teachings of The *Sacred 7*.

You see, this powerful form of introduction is not only meant to establish birth and identity in those who speak it, but it's also meant to break down the concepts and illusions that are given in childhood and that are embellished through the human experience. The metaphysical concepts are used as energetic building blocks that empower you, rather than to create some sort of opposition to break through the captivity of the past. You discover that, within the container of your identity, lies a profound vehicle for self-realization, understanding, and ultimately spiritual power. The process helps to limit the suggestive nature of a culture that processes people like a factory and helps you build an identity that is synonymous with your true self.

As you go through the process of constructing your own *Sacred 7*, and as many of your limiting *I AM* statements begin to fall away, you may find it challenging to let go of them. Inside your mindscape, your egoic mind has constructed and fortified a place of hiding. It has comforted you with a blanket of thoughts all about doing more, achieving more, and being rewarded more. If you're like most of the rest of us, that childish blanket is beyond filthy, yet it is still warm. it has become soiled with the emptiness of success or failure, victory or victimization. As you journey with The *Sacred 7*, I will encourage you, as I have done for myself, to see it through, to be patient, and to love yourself. By doing so, you will begin to understand that you have an opportunity to experience more of your life and manifest more in your emotional, spiritual, and physical world than you've ever thought possible. As you practice this technology, more of the true meaning of your existence will unfold within you.

***

The Seven Sacred Containers of Self-Identity lets you know deep within you that you're already something. You've already arrived. It opens the portal to your connection to the lands of your ancestors, which has created the metaphysical architecture for who you are. In these days of polarity, anger, and distrust, it's imperative to know this. You can begin to see that you're like a tree, rooted in the deep ground of your ancestry, planted near a life-giving stream that feeds your quest for successful and powerful spiritual living.

The *Sacred 7* can shift us from coming from a place of separation to being relational again. It allows anybody to apply it and begin to establish connections with the *air, water, fire, and earth*. It begins simply enough. I watch people in a circle, in front of a fire, introducing themselves to the fire, introducing themselves to the river, introducing themselves to the wind, and discovering themselves there. I watch people reclaim that they are connected to gravity, time, and Spirit. For them, it becomes a foundation for stepping back into the earthling experience with an open heart and a reclaimed self.

From these relationships, you can begin to know yourself without the confusion of a culture that is more focused on creating jobs than fulfilled human beings. For the first time, you might find comfort in listening to the drum of your heartbeat, the softness of the wind through your hair, or the warmth of the sun against your skin. You might feel as if this whole world was created for you. If you step into the process, hold tight—it gets better, deeper, and even more insightful.

Let me help you find your *Sacred 7*. It will help you reestablish your relationships, reconcile the meaning of this incarnation, and learn to live with meaningful purpose. The *Sacred 7* is a foundation for so much that your heart yearns for. it is a way to place your feet firmly upon the Earth and launch yourself into a world of deep ceremonial significance. Your *Sacred 7* is a homecoming.

Welcome home.

CHAPTER 5

THE SEVEN SACRED CONTAINERS

When we introduce ourselves to others, it's assumed that we know the person we are introducing. But who is it that we know ourselves to be? Who have we come to believe that we are? If we scratch below the thin surface of quickly-tossed Hello's and How-are-ya's, most of us live lives within the confinement of an identity that has been weaved together by self-imposed beliefs and limitations, community expectations, and cultural perceptions.

The Sacred 7 offers us a time-tested tool to redeem our identity and reshape it back into wholeness. It allows us to intentionally create ourselves energetically in relationship to what is within the story of ourselves. We learn to hold space for identity in new, empowered ways that help to wash away the confusion of the illusions created by the traumas of our life experience. As most of us live within inherited and self-constructed wounded identities, The Sacred 7 provides us a means to build a fortified *metaphysical architecture*— a conscious and meaningful construct of our identity—to bring out our highest ways of being. It introduces us to the ideals for our relationships with ourselves, others, and all of life and provides metaphoric and energetic resources to embody them. It gives us the means to shape the perceptions we choose to have about ourselves and the world and come into alignment with the highest principles of our divine architecture.

What we are taught, what we accept, and what we hold as truth about ourselves can run like an unseen, viral program within the many layers of ourselves. Emotional triggers and dense feelings from our human experience can overload us. So we spend our lives waiting for the perfect relationship, waiting for the perfect job, waiting for discovery of the meaning of existence. We wait in frustration because those things never come. We wait until isolation and captivity become the norm. At times, we can even become comfortable within the confusion that is given to us by a system that has all but forgotten the traditions of our global tribal ancestors.

The Sacred 7 is built on the ancestral connection that once was a part of humanity's understanding of itself. The confusion brought on by the great illusion of self— of not knowing who you are—is dissolved within the groundedness and clarity of *The Sacred 7*. You and you alone are responsible for molding and creating the energetic manifestation of who you are to serve your optimal design.

THE SEVEN SACRED CONTAINERS

***

The Sacred 7 is comprised of seven energetic containers that hold the space for our self-realization and the highest expression of the most potent aspects of ourselves. They are tools to connect with our deepest wisdom and to free ourselves from the limitations of an unconsciously-constructed identity. Each one is unique and powerful. Each one helps us transmute the trauma we have held within that distinct aspect of ourselves and eventually become a vehicle through which we can access our authenticity and act with grace and love in the world.

Each of *The Sacred 7* containers also embody a higher and broader perception, a lens through which we can see ourselves and the world and build a healthy relationship with ourselves. For each of the seven containers, we can ask ourselves: *Am I being intentional about this perception? Am I holding enough love for myself in relationship to that energy?* We can also ask: *Am I loosening myself from any captivity I experience within this perception of myself—enough so that I can reconnect with my own sovereignty?*

The technology of *The Sacred 7* containers takes patience to adopt. Like anything profound and meaningful, more is revealed to you as you practice your introduction and grow with the teachings of this ancient view of life.

***

My time in prison was a time of deep cognitive and spiritual redemption, but there still remained a feeling of lack within myself. The many books I read opened me up to the idea that I could step into living parts of myself and begin to heal what was hurting, fill what was missing, and build what was weak within me. I learned to transform much of my trauma into medicine.

It was there that I first began to understand that I could reshape the pain of childhood. As I began to work on healing my past, I discovered one of the viral programs locked within the matrix of my mind: the shame that had been and continued to spill over into virtually every aspect of my life. That childhood shame brought me to crime, alcoholism, and ultimately, heroin addiction. The first download of it came when I was nine years old. I had been caught shoplifting at the Fred Myer department store in my neighborhood in Portland, Oregon, and my stepfather came to pick me up. My mom wasn't allowed in the store because she had been caught stealing there already, so it was my stepfather who came for me. I had been stealing some toys, just as my mom had taught me to, when a plainclothes security guard grabbed me and carried me, fighting and screaming, through the store. I was paralyzed with fear at the thought of being put into state custody. My mom had drilled it into my mind that if I was ever caught, I would be taken by the state. They took my picture and processed some paperwork. Yet as my stepfather walked me out the door, he proclaimed that I had popped my cherry and insisted that I had done good.

Once in the car, I had to face my mom. She looked at me and asked me if I had learned to steal from her. Deeply fearful and afraid that, if I said I had, she wouldn't take me to steal with her anymore, I lied to her. Our shoplifting trips had been one of the few ways we could be together and I craved time with her. So, I balled up my shame and told her, No, It wasn't her fault.

It wasn't until prison that I felt safe enough to challenge myself to heal this deep wound of shame. For me, prison was a safe place. Ironically, after 25 years of fear and insecurity at "home," it was my three years in prison that gave me more of a sense of protection and safety than I had felt in a long time. I carved out some time to allow myself to go back in time to the very moment of my shame. I walked myself through the process. I sat down and remembered the smells of beer, the cigarettes, and the alcohol in the car. I remembered the way the floor felt, and I remembered my own smell because I was so afraid that I'd gone to the bathroom on myself. As I reviewed the experience and became present to it the voice of what I would now call the *Divine Masculine* arose. It was the metaphysical architecture of my own father protecting me from the shameful words of my mother and nurturing the child within me. As I walked myself gently through the experience, I was able to boldly tell my mother the truth: that I did learn to steal from her and that, yes, she could have taught me better.

That experience of forging my own healing process would emerge as *The Sacred 7* and guide the direction of the process I've learned and refined over the years. *The Sacred 7* has guided me to go even deeper into the past and recast the parts of myself into wholeness. Instead of just being the child in the back seat of the car, for example, I have learned to be my own mom and to say to that child, *I love you*—the words that child needed to hear. *The Sacred 7* allows you to transform each of the seven relational aspects of yourself into wholeness.

***

The Seven Sacred Containers are seven sacred aspects of yourself. As stated earlier, they consist of you, your mother, your father, your mother's mother, your father's mother, your mother's father, and your father's father. Each container is associated with a direction:. These directions open us up to a greater perception of ourselves through their own energetic identity. Many indigenous spiritual teachings have at their center a call to the directions to help place people in a framework of spiritually perceiving life. Since the directions are intangible and boundary-less, we just dive into them their vastness, knowing that the journey is enough to give our steps more certainty.

The directions remind us that life is not fully comprehended until it is seen from a more expansive perspective. They are a remedy to our habit of only seeing one side of ourselves and an antidote to our captivity to the trauma we've experienced. It is so easy—in fact, extraordinarily common—for us to get caught up in one or two particular ways of seeing ourselves, ways that are narrow, confining, and usually self-critical. When we observe the experiences of what we once called trauma and abuse from the broader perspective of the directions, we are able to let go of the bondage to those experiences and finally find peace. The directions give us the ability to process and define our history in a way that serves us.

The Seven Containers and their directions work in conjunction with one another to help make visible the blind spots of your consciousness. It's why this practice is so important. It allows us to view ourselves from a relational standpoint like those of the ancient tribal people of the world who intuitively see all things as connected, vibrant, and perfect. As you practice The Sacred 7 you unleash the power of the optimal state of your own human design.

THE SEVEN SACRED CONTAINERS

Now let's look into the energies and intentions of all of *The Sacred 7 Containers of Self-Identity*. Here I describe their essence and energy, the intention and possibility within each container and direction. In the next chapter, I'll describe how to construct and work with your own *Sacred 7 Containers* of *Self-Identity* so you can begin to birth a new metaphysical architecture for yourself that hastens and supports your true spiritual freedom.

We begin with the first three containers of self-identity: the trinity of self, mother, and father.

The child part of us represents the sacred place, the truest truth of the truth that we know. It represents the playful, whimsical, inspiring part of us that knows how to have fun and feel good. The next two containers—the mother and father—represent our internalized parental energies and the opportunity to parent ourselves to wholeness. I created the *metaphysical architectures* of these identities, formulated around the *Divine Feminine* and *Divine Masculine*, to serve me in my own healing process. They will take you from questioning why you were born into your family to the deep knowing that the purposes of the universe are timeless and revelatory.

These three, *Sacred Child* and *Divine Mother* and *Divine Father* form the fundamentals of our identity. All three work together for us to live life with a sense of freedom. If our own mother and father aspects are in full flower, our *inner child* flourishes. That gives us the freedom to playfully dance, to unselfconsciously sing, and to explore new places, new people, and new ideas in life. It allows us to be our authentic self. Our inner *Divine Feminine* and *Divine Masculine* know instinctively when our *sacred inner self* needs to be nurtured and protected through an experience of life. And when they are free to provide that sustenance, you feel you are fed and nourished enough internally. It's when you know that your environment is safe enough to open to the oneness with your truest self.

Being intentional with your *inner child*, your *Divine Feminine*, and your *Divine Masculine* aspects, you will find the strength of the *Trinity*. You will find a deeper sense of freedom and emotional sovereignty than you have ever experienced. It is this that leads to a powerful life.

The Sacred Child The Inside place The Inner Child

As mentioned above, the first sacred container is the child within, the *Sacred Child*. This *magical* and *sacred* part of you is important to protect and embrace. It is *you*. It is represented by the direction of *Inside*. It represents the free, innocent, spontaneous, loving and God-conscious part of ourselves. We all have this part within us.

Our *inner child* is often where we hold our sense of victimhood. By working with your *Sacred Child* container, you can move from victimhood to sovereignty. It can help you unlock the stored energy within the experience of your victimhood to be a powerful, limitless being. It can transmute it from a dense weight holding you back into an energetic empowerment that pushes you forward into a life filled with love and gratitude.

It's important to understand that a victim's feelings—as unlikeable and painful as they may be—are powerful, and their energy can be used to help you in your spiritual path of becoming who you want to be. Once transformed, the victim, when combined with authenticity and vulnerability, can expand your empathic response and deepen your connection to your truth. That power will also support you in the development of the next six containers of self-identity.

Understanding your *inner child* takes looking into the feelings you had within you when you stopped being free enough to play, when fear, addiction, and suffering began to rob you of the practice of playful magic. Growing up the way I did, finding my way to the path of violence and drug dealing, there were many times when I could look back and say that the child within me was lost. And although there are many stories of beauty in my life, the one that I've had to rewrite to be able to travel into the past and proclaim my power was when I was just a child. It was a very early memory of mine.

It was a cold day in Portland, and I was bundled in my winter jacket stuffed tightly with my hood and beany cap keeping me warm. I remember the car. The floorboard was rusted out so we would throw pieces of trash out the holes as we drove down the road. I was so happy to be in the car with my mom, listening to the radio, exploring the world. Since it was close to lunchtime, my mom stopped to get us a bucket of chicken. She gave me the warm bucket of food to sit in my lap, as it smelled like only Kentucky Fried Chicken can smell. I was so happy then. She drove us over to a park where we got out and she walked me over to an empty playground. She looked at me and said, *Mommy has to leave for a minute. I will be right back. Be a big boy and just stay here and have some chicken.* I was about seven years old.

School had taught us about stranger danger so, to me, every car that passed was a potential kidnapper. The sounds in the park seemed to get louder and I was launched into a full-on panic. I remember stuffing the chicken into my mouth, feeding the loss of my mom with a substance. It was the first time that addiction came into my life. It wasn't heroin, it wasn't alcohol, it was food. More importantly, it was the first time I traded substance for relationship and the first time I had to be a big boy and tell myself that I couldn't be a child. It was the first time the imbalance of my *Divine Masculine* took over to protect me. It was the first time the *illusion of separation* from my own *divine child* happened for me.

Divine Feminine The Below direction The Nurturer

The Below direction contains the nurturing qualities of the *Divine Feminine*, there to invite into your reality. Within the Below space are the qualities that will nurture you throughout the next five containers. It is the deep-rooted darkness that, when embraced, has the potential to bring forth life. It has always been the birthing place. it has always been the place of foundations. It will be present with you in all aspects of your life, helping you be courageous enough to look at yourself.

The *metaphysical architecture* of your biological mother holds the space of your *Divine Feminine* and nurturing capacity in this life. (If you don't know your biological mother, you can still work with this space powerfully. The details are offered in Chapter 6.) She represents the *Divine Feminine* and represents how you relate to that energy in your relationship to yourself. This is most important because without the embrace of the energetic qualities of your own personal *Divine Feminine*, the *child within* does not gain the perspective of seeing itself with the eyes of the nurturer.

Some may find it difficult to see the *Divine Feminine* presence in their own mother. Understand that your mother was brought into this reality by you. You can ask yourself: *What have I done to learn from her? What medicine has she hidden in the darkness of the Below space for me to birth into power?* Remember, it is your choice to fortify the *metaphysical architecture* for the *Divine Feminine*. It is your freedom to not be held captive by her voice but to become her voice instead. The field in which you develop the *Divine Feminine* is vast as darkness itself.

As the one who nurtures us, the *Divine Feminine* is there for the *inner child* within us. She is the one that kisses the knee with the boo boo on it and reassures us that it's going to be okay. Some of us lost this connection to ourselves when our mother's inability to nurture us created a lack within ourselves. For many of us, this happened at a young age and created a vibrational field of neglect within ourselves. The emotional loss affected our system and we decided that the pain of offering our hurt to an absent *Divine Feminine* wasn't worth connecting to the nurturing aspect of ourselves. In that vacuum, we lost a part ourselves that was vital to living a whole and complete life.

When we mature through *The Sacred 7* and intentionally fortify this aspect of ourselves, when we are able to kiss our wounds ourselves and discover a new empowered relationship with our ability to provide for our own needs. This feminine aspect gives our *inner child* what it needs to feel attended to. It provides a nurturing foundation for us, built from within, that allows us to create and experience deep intimacy and healthy relationships. It opens us up empathetically and connects us to others with vulnerability. And that nourishes the power of our authenticity.

It's not surprising that many of us feel a void inside. Maybe as a child, you needed someone to be there for you but your mother went to work every day. Maybe that energy of nurturing was absent. Maybe your mom worked 9 to 5 in order to make ends meet, and she was absent for a lot of your life. Our culture, of course, has its hyper-focus on jobs rather than people, so your mom may have, in her own life, been nothing more than victim to an oppressive system of captivity. Yet because of the system's obsession with the victim, you may not ever be able to see that until you practice *The Sacred 7*.

When we bring attention to the *Divine Feminine* aspect of ourselves, we're able to take responsibility for our lives and in essence, become our own mother. If we haven't learned it by experiencing it, then we have to practice it. To take responsibility for it, we can ask ourselves, *How can I go in deeply to the need within myself and facilitate the transformation of that dense energy into a process that serves me, my family, and my community? If I need that nurturing, how can I provide that for myself? How can I be that representation of myself for myself?* Tapping into our connection to the *Divine Feminine* from the perspective of the Below space offers us an infinite playground to work out the process of transforming this part of ourselves. We can go back to that first boo boo, when Mom didn't have the time to kiss it okay, or when mom's breast wasn't available when we needed food, and we can give ourselves what we need. We can be emboldened with the courage to look within ourselves and examine what our own needs are. By doing so, we nurture ourselves, and we are able to nurture others.

That's what it did for me. Witnessing my mother's life has equipped me with a deep sense of empathy for those who are caught in the throes of addiction. Even more came from learning how to love her even in her state of self-destruction. I remember one night vividly. I had returned to Portland at the age of 18, many years after the separation from my mom had left a longing for the love that only a mother can give. She and I were watching TV in her one-bedroom apartment in the projects of Portland, Oregon when the door flew open and a man that was high on methamphetamine pushed himself in. He crawled into a corner and cowered there, saying something about Hell's Angels chasing after him. I jumped up from the couch and looked for something to defend our home with—maybe a piece of wood or a stick—something I could hit the guy with. But my mother calmed me down and began to reach out for the guy. He was struggling in his mental illness and was in a place of complete and utter paranoia. She went over to him and asked him what he had taken. He wasn't able to tell her. He just told her to listen for the sound of the motorcycles. She told him she couldn't hear them and just looked at him with her beautiful brown eyes.

In that moment, I felt some sort of energy in the room, some sort of medicine enter into the experience. My mom walked over to the refrigerator, poured the guy a glass of milk, and stood there with him until he took it from her. Still scared and frightened, he began to drink the milk as she told him about the times when she had done too much methamphetamine or cocaine and had been completely paranoid and embarrassed herself. She talked about times that she had done things that brought shame to her and her family. She sat with that man in our home. The fear inside me began to melt and I started to see my mother as a medicine woman. I started to recognize her ministry and see that she was more than what the world had told me she was. I started to see her as a loving person who very much cared about those she was drawn to serve.

This kind of event was a common theme in my mom's life. She had rescued a prostitute named Maria, whom we met when we were selling stolen merch for a drug dealer. Maria's face was red and swollen from her pimp's beatings. My mother told Maria that she could teach her a way that she could hustle without having to sell her body. She told her that she could teach her to steal and to shoplift and that she could join a crew and make real money. After that, Maria and my mom grew close and Maria would often show up at the house to go shoplifting with my mom.

Most people find it difficult to understand, but the life of an addict can at times exhibit tremendous beauty. When my mom died from an overdose, my uncle told us that she had wasted her life. Maybe he said that to send a message to my sister, my young cousins, and me when we showed up at the funeral. I am sure that he had good intentions, though his words left me paralyzed with anger. Yet, there were others that had other thoughts. At her funeral, a man who had slept on our floor in the projects told me that my mom had always fed him when he was hungry and gave him a place to sleep when he needed it. Not many people have a homeless, addicted man show up at their funeral. My mom had made such a connection with him that he shared in our grief and taught us all about the love that a woman shared with the people she cared for.

From my mother's teachings, I was able to formulate an architecture around the *Divine Feminine* to serve my process. I don't think about my mother in a way that most people think about theirs. I don't think about the trauma anymore; I don't think about the pain that her decisions caused in a way that victimizes me anymore. Instead, I think about her in a way that serves my process and through that, I find gratitude and a relationship with her. That gratitude has led me to a deep understanding of the medicine road that I've been given. If it wasn't for my mother's teachings, I don't think I would be able to sit with the people in psychiatric lockdowns or drug rehabs that I do drum circles with and look at them and lovingly say to them, *I see my mother in your eyes.* I am now gifted to see the nurturing of the *Divine Feminine* through my mother in my life.

The gift that our moms give to us is sometimes hidden in their neglect. If we don't free ourselves from the pain, we'll never learn to use those feelings to help us serve others, and by doing so, serve ourselves. When I feel that deep sense of connecting to another human being through my trauma, I feel a deep sense of gratitude. It's a gratitude that has led me to ask the *Great Spirit* how many times my mother was raped in a drug house or beaten by the police. It gives me empathy and connection, which in turn give me freedom.

You can do the same kind of thing yourself and transform hurt, abandonment, or anger into love and gratitude as you commune with your *Divine Feminine* in the *Below* space. As you practice the technology of The Sacred 7, the chains that once bound you to your victim will become the fuel for the fire that you dance around. And you might actually find the medicine your mom provides you by empowering you to kiss your own boo boo's.

Divine Masculine The Above direction The Protector

Safety is a major need for all of us. When we grow up feeling unsafe, every aspect of our lives can be affected. The domain of the *Divine Masculine* is all about creating safe space through conscious protection. To my indigenous ancestors, the masculine side of ourselves is the one responsible for this protection. If the *Divine Masculine* is absent as the protector and keeper of our security, we become afraid to live life, we lose our voice, and we become powerless to the sometimes cruel influences of the world. In the world we grew up in, we may have been teased or called names and no one stood up for us or pushed back at the bullies. It may have been easy to get punished for things we didn't do; or not have our side of the story told. The feeling of being unshielded from the world turns into imbalance within ourselves.

The truth is, many of our fathers weren't protected themselves; they were traumatized, and their own *Divine Masculine* side was not fortified. They may have mistakenly elevated the system or their culture into the role of protector; or even worse, they may have been abused themselves and so they never learned to be any sort of protector for anyone else. As their offspring, as young bystanders, the child within us grows up feeling unsheltered and insecure. If you never felt protected, you never felt safe. If you don't feel safe, you're not going to live an abundant life.

The container of the *Divine Masculine* is the protector, the action force of life. He is *Father Sky* and the place of the *Divine Light*. This aspect of ourselves brings to us a sense of protection and safety and provides the logical analytical side. By owning this aspect and working with this container, we can ask ourselves, *What do I need to do to create a sense of protection for myself. How do I learn to feel the sensation of safety for myself?*

An imbalance in our *Divine Masculine* can lead to a life of missed opportunities. The *Divine Masculine* is the aspect of your optimal self that creates a field of confidence. Think about the times when you've been in line at the grocery store, and there was something intuitive inside you propelling you to talk to the person you're in line with. How often did you respond to it? You might have wanted to reach out and say a friendly Hello, but if you didn't feel safe internally, you might have browsed your phone instead of making eye contact. Likewise, if you're in a business meeting and have something to add but you just don't feel safe, you won't take the risk and you or your company may suffer as a result.

If you don't feel secure and protected and you suppress your inspired ideas, you're going to miss opportunities. Maybe that person in the grocery store was going to offer you a job opportunity or introduce you to the person you'll fall in love with. Or maybe she has a spiritual insight for you that could transform your life in your community. With the protection, the child inside of us feels safe to risk and free to really play.

My own father was a true criminal, and, yes, he was a thief. But in my neighborhood, my father was a well-respected man. He would walk into any home of any drug dealer and be honored with a place to sit. He earned the respect of many. Which is why, in our neighborhood, he was known as Robin Hood.

My dad lived the last years of his life in a truck camper in the backyard of my grandparents' house, sick with Hep C. I had been selling drugs in the neighborhood for a couple years, and my dad was one of my customers. One night, I brought him a bag of weed and we sat there smoking a joint and talking. As we sat there, he told me that he knew that one way or another, I was going to end up in prison. He knew where the lifestyle was leading me to. He could see the outcome. And of course, he was right. He told me to promise him that I would stay away from the gangs, that I wouldn't do drugs in prison, that I would watch who I owed money to, watch who I lent money to, and not gamble. He said if I did those things I would stay safe. He told me nobody gets hurt in prison for no reason, nobody gets raped in prison for no reason, and everything that's done in prison is done for a reason. As long as I kept to myself, he said, I would be fine. He told me to find someone my age that I could trust and hang out with. Keep my circle of friends small, he told me, and always look out for those they called themselves my friend.

For a few years after my dad said those words to me, I moved in and out of a victim mentality. My first reaction was to think that he was such a horrible father that all he could do was to tell me that I was going to prison. Pure victim.

But eventually I saw that if I stayed in that victim perspective—which has some truth to it, after all—I might not see the bigger picture. I wouldn't get to see what the *Creator* wanted me to see. Turns out, my father's words are probably the reason that I am not a career criminal—or dead—today. Through his kind words and mentorship, I was able to survive one of the most dangerous decades in American history: the nineties. It is because of him, I made it out of gang-infested neighborhoods, out of the gun battles, the drug deals, and the close calls with death. His words are, and forever will be, a part of me.

This is the power of the representation of the *Divine Masculine*. This is how my father's identity is a part of my *Sacred 7* process and how I have created a story around my father that serves me today.

Mother's mother The East Who you are to new people

In the East we find the dawning of the sun; it is where the new day is born. In *The Sacred 7*, the energy of the *East* is expressed through our mother's mother as she holds space for the new relationships that come into our lives. Our mother's mother is the guardian of that space and holds that perspective for us as we need it. She allows us to view ourselves through her in the place of the East.

The East is the place where we build the emerging idea of who we are. It's where we gain a powerful perspective to loosen ourselves from the captivity of the old and embrace the *newness of life.*

Every relationship is new at some point. From the perspective of the East, we stand in our authenticity, and we stand open to new relationships that make their way to us. We're open to meeting new friends, finding a new job, or experience new members of our community. But when we have an imbalance in this aspect of ourselves, we're sluggish to begin new relationships and shy away from them, often to the detriment of our self-expression and our ability to give and receive connection with others. We escape new relationships by isolating ourselves.

Your mother's mother holds space for us to be open to new things. Her outstretched hand is saying, *This is who you are to new people.* She helps you define who you are in that space. Again, The Sacred 7 offers you perceptions to step into, a *metaphysical architecture* to construct by choice. No matter how you might wish others to perceive you, whatever perceptions you hold for yourself is what others will see. For example, if I perceive myself to be a loser, a drug addict or a criminal, then that's what others will see in me. But as I build and reflect back to them the energetic architecture of who I choose to be to new people, through the gentle space held by my mother's mother, then my heart opens and so does theirs.

My mother's mother was Elva Gallegos. Within the ancient technology of tribal introduction, the mother's mother is the clan in which you are born. This association to the feminine is a pragmatic way of understanding one's own clan and fits into a genetic pattern that is more associated with our actual DNA. In other words, all of us are more of our mother and she's more of her mother, and that's why most tribal communities look at the matriarchal as the line of lineage. That's why I believe my *Apache* ancestors looked to the mother's side. This paradigm is true for many of the original indigenous systems of identity, a matriarchal system that honors the feminine.

I am born from the ancestors of my grandmother, the *Apache* people of West Texas. We had many different clan names. So, through my research, I have found a connection to the *Lipanese* or the *Lipan Apache*. When I was a child, my grandma would sing me her Spanish songs and tell me the stories of the mystical encounters that the people of our ancestors had with *God*. She was the first to show me unconditional love. She never tried to correct my behavior or tell me that I needed to study harder. She never tried to tell me that I wasn't smart enough in school or tried to judge my report cards. She simply would say to me that I was loved and that she loved me.

She lived near White Sands, New Mexico, in a little town named Capitan, right outside the *Mescalero Reservation* in Lincoln County. It got most of its fame for being one of the hideouts of the famous American outlaw, Billy the Kid.

Her house was situated close to the military base where the United States government tested nuclear bombs and would light up when the bombs went off like a flash from a camera. By the time I knew her, her body had been torn apart by cancer. She'd lost her breast, her arm was swollen, and she was suffering from many other problems. But she never complained. She only smiled and said things were okay. My grandmother was a powerful representation of my own identity. She lived through so much and never once showed me anything but real faith. At night we would pray the "Our Father" and "Hail Mary" together. She taught me to have a relationship with something greater than myself.

Now, in her position in my *Sacred 7*, she holds a powerful space for me to show the world around me that I'm fine and that I can continue to love even through my own suffering. I thank my grandmother for taking on those aspects of myself in order to teach me how to love others. I thank her for coming into this world as a mother, as a grandmother, as a wife, as a teacher. She will always be a powerful representation of my own self. She is the representation of who I am to new people.

By reliving the stories of my grandmother and sharing them, I am fortifying the energetic displacement and manifestation of her as a guardian for me. Spiritually, she lives in the unseen parts of reality even though she has been gone physically for years. When she comes through to teach me, I know her voice because I have built a relationship with her. I can feel her in my life because I know her. If you don't know your grandparents, it doesn't mean that they don't exist. Most of us can hold the container to find the relationship. Look to the *East* to call your grandma and listen to find her voice. Once you hear it, you will always know she is there.

The Father's Mother The South Who you are to your family

How are you intentionally creating the experience of your family? How are you opening your heart to them? There's often a language we have with our family, like the way we set the table or gather for holidays. And individually, there's a whole concept that we hold around who we are in our family. The Father's Mother aspect of our *Sacred 7* helps us intentionally create who we choose to be in our family.

My family firmly believed that the apple doesn't fall too far from the tree. It held an imposing *metaphysical architecture* that colored my family's perceptions of me, convincing them that they knew who I was and who I will always be. Even after being clean for seven years, I would still feel behaviors come up inside myself that fell within the fortified space that my family was holding for me. But I understood where they were coming from. The reality was that they had been deeply hurt by all the times I had told them I was not going back to crime or that I was going to get clean, and I didn't. They had believed in me, trusted in me, and then I went out and used anyway. They didn't want to risk their hopes and love on me again only to be hurt and disappointed for the millionth time. My family had also been affected by my parents and what they had done to them over the years. So, they created barriers and walls and fortified a space of my identity. To free myself from that, I needed to strengthen myself to be around my family. I needed to strengthen who I was in the conceptualization of my identity, the "Andrew" to them, and I did so by intentionally re-building my father's mother container—my relationship to my family. I knew that things were shifting when I noticed that the family began to recognize me as the person who said the prayers at the family meals. It was a huge step for me. I knew that in the eyes of my family I was finally being seen as a spiritual person rather than a criminal drug addict.

My father's mother, Evelyn Beatty, is a Scotch-Irish woman from Pennsylvania. She has an extremely strong work ethic and holds the space of strong perfection and providing for her family. When she was young, she made dozens of cookies to feed our family and the neighborhood kids. She taught me games and she taught me ways of playing. She was always open to sharing a card deck or board game. She instilled in me the sense that the family is a powerful place of self-realization.

She taught me what it means to work hard, to dedicate yourself to perfection and to process life in a way that creates a system of organization. She's the reason that I don't leave the house without making my bed. The metaphysical architecture of my father's mother in my life holds space for who I am as a son, a cousin, a brother, a father, a grandfather, and an uncle. I thank her for the deepest teachings that she gave me when I was a lost child suffering from post-traumatic stress and completely hurting inside. She was the first person to send me to group therapy. She brought me to an Al-Anon meeting when I was in the eighth grade, which helped me begin to make a little sense of my life.

As a primary aspect of myself, my father's mother holds space for the ideal representation of who I am to my family. When I name my father's mother in my introduction, I am saying to the world around me that I am holding space for my higher self to resonate in a frequency that serves my relationship to my family.

Andrew Wayne, Thomas Ecker

Mother's Father The West Who you are to your community

The place of your mother's father has to do with your relationship to your *community: who you are in relationship to your friends, your job, your place of worship, and your tribe.* It asks of you, *How are you perceiving yourself in relationship to your community? How are you intentionally creating your sense of who you are in relationship to the groups of people you choose to have in your life?*

Are we holding enough love for ourselves that even when others oppose or try to diminish us, we can maintain our sense of love and protection in the face of it? If we really want to establish this identity, we need to ask this question. In community, we are called to be present with the world outside of our family and outside of our comfort zone. At times, we are called to speak the truth of the voice of love. If we fortify this space, we are most likely to speak up when the culture around us turns from love to fear and hate, and when it expresses itself in racism and separation. A fortified concept of community-self, in its perspective from the West, helps us see that we can express a greater calling of our lives and serve with love and acceptance. It is the power to speak up when the voices of intolerance yell with fear and separation into our ears.

If you know who you are to community, you will prevail. The great spiritual teachers have always found strength in their identity as it is reflected within community. When we look into this perspective we can find a deep sense of mission and profound determination to equip our fellow members of community with a foundation to live a better life and to be greater representations of the divine cause of love.

Since I had been bounced around so many times in my childhood from family member to family member, my experience of who I was in the family was very insecure. My relationship to community got out of balance and disconnected, which is one reason I gravitated towards the criminal lifestyle. In the criminal community, I finally felt I was in a place that didn't hold judgment over me. My own family, on the other hand, seemed to constantly judge me about my grades, my work ethic, how I wore my clothes, and seemingly everything else. With all that, community started to become more important to me than my own family.

My mother's father, Leroy Lindsay, told me he was *Apache* and either English or Scotch. He would say that was why he couldn't grow a beard and didn't have any hair on his chest. He was the toughest man I have ever met in my life and taught me so much. Back in Portland, when I came home from school after being asked by the kids on the playground what race I was, he was the one I went to with this profound question. The smell of cigarettes hung in the kitchen air when I sat down at our small coffee table. He sat there, as usual, with a bottle of cheap whiskey and a cigarette dangling from the side of his mouth. He dressed like a cowboy with a beaver fur cowboy hat, straight leg Levi jeans, and a western shirt with at least one pocket for his tobacco. A slim man, he wore a thick belt around his waist to keep his pants on and kept an old-timer, razor-sharp knife at his side. Both the knife and his belt would turn into weapons when he needed them. I had seen him pull off his belt, wrap it around his big fist, and chase one of my mom's hippie-type drug-addicted friends who had worn out their welcome or been rude out of his house. Seeing my 86-year-old grandfather chase after someone with a belt wrapped around his hand was often funny to me and just a part of growing up the way we did.

Confused and perplexed from the day at school, I sought him out for answers about my heritage. He told me to tell the kids at school I was a renegade Apache Indian. His words left a lasting impression on me.

Leroy grew up in rural Arkansas, the oldest of five brothers and sisters. He was still quite young when his father died, and he was left to care for his family since that was what the oldest boy did back then. He was a man of many travels and a different type of man as many of the older generations are. I once watched him perform oral surgery on himself with a pair of plyers. On rare occasion, when he got cut on a job, instead of going to the doctor for stitches, he'd simple duct-tape himself and get back to work. When he was 16 and times got hard for his family, he signed up for the Navy by falsifying the family Bible. He went from shooting squirrels with a .22 caliber rifle in Arkansas to being on a Navy destroyer in the middle of the Korean war. He served in the Navy for 23 years and his stories still live on in my heart.

My grandfather brought home with him a lot of the pain of serving his country through so much war. There were times when, after a late night of drinking, he would wake me up to show me what the Viet Cong would do to soldiers. He'd push my fingers back until I cried and hold me down as I tried to fight him off until I went to the bathroom on myself. It was his way of trying to make me a man. I look back at those times now and see his suffering in his alcoholism and I feel the pain of what he must have gone through to be able to do that to his grandson.

I lived with this grandfather for almost two years in

THE SEVEN SACRED CONTAINERS

Arkansas after my mom went back to prison. The time I spent in the hills with him in his childhood home were some of the most transformative years of my life. We lived in a small house on 40 acres that could have been on 4000 acres because there was really nothing around us. I learned to hunt and fish, farm and raise chickens, and trap. In the summertime, our well went dry and I had to climb the mountain with two five-gallon buckets in hand to bring water back to our house. Life there wasn't easy. We didn't have plumbing of any kind and cooked on a very primitive wood-burning stove. We cut our own wood for the winter and we ate rabbits and squirrels and hunted and fished.

I learned a lot about myself and my grandfather during that time. His disease of alcoholism progressed while I was there and it wasn't long before he was back to drinking cheap vodka and a case of beer a day. After all of the alcohol and abuse, I am still able to find my love for my grandfather and hold his choices within that love. I've learned to love him and not hold those actions against him. The experiences that he provided me in Arkansas are ones that will forever remain a huge part of who I am. From him, I've learned that choosing to see our experiences beyond good or bad gives us the ability to find freedom. Through loving myself enough to find the medicine in my relationship with my grandfather, I have found a place in which I can see that he sacrificed so much of himself to be of service to his community. Even his ability to function without alcohol. I have found peace in this lesson and I have learned to hold space for myself to serve community through him.

The idea of serving the community is extremely important when you're in the process of finding your own medicine.

It is through this intention that I can actually see myself in the embodiment of my mother's father. There were times when my grandfather's love felt abusive and hard. It felt as though he was trying to create the man that he had to be at a young age inside of the boy that I was. Because of that, I have had to destroy and recreate my relationship with my grandfather many times in my life in order to create the energetic displacement and manifestation within my own reality. The process of destruction and birthing has led me to create an identity that helps me come to grips with the way that he loved me. It helped me let go of the blame, shame, and guilt associated with the words that he said to me and the shame that he put upon me for the actions of my mother.

In creating a relationship with my grandfather, I have found a deep empathetic connection with the people who have served in the military and what it means to sacrifice for community and country.

Father's Father The North Who you are to nature, the planet, and the elements

All the work that we've done with *The Sacred 7* to this point—through healing our relationships with ourselves, our parents, our family and community—brings us to the point where we can be vulnerable and caring enough to the environment and animals and trees to care about them. The empathetic response and ability to be vulnerable in human relationships transfers to bringing it to our relationships to nature, sky, environment. The identity of the father's father Is the perspective of the *North*. When we intentionally fortify this aspect of ourselves, we harness the ability to be one with everything that is governed by the elements—*the air, water, fire, and earth.* From this perspective, we discover what it means to have a relationship with the animals and to see ourselves in them as they pass through our reality. We can ask questions of the Creator: *Why did you send the black bird? Why is the deer looking at me? What is the meaning of the direction of the wind?*

Since the father's father holds huge space for connection with what is outside of human relationships, we may feel a distance to this aspect of ourselves. Nevertheless, rest assured that with practice the essence of this space will come through like a voice calling you to the expanse of your consciousness. As we practice the harnessing of the *metaphysical architecture* of this perspective of self, we learn that the nature of our human experience is beyond the boundaries and limits of communication. The sound of the crackling fire becomes a part of the ecosystem of your mind. You grow your ability to relate to all things.

My father's father, Wayne Ecker, German and Algonquin, from Pennsylvania. I spent many hours with him in a tiny fishing boat on the lakes of Arizona. He taught me to fish and to enjoy nature. He taught me to harvest the fish and clean them and to respect the fish as a provision for our family.

He was a man of gentle heart. He loved to experience the warmth of the sunrise overlooking the lake. He was at his best when he was enjoying the outdoors among the great trees, the grasses, and the beauty. He taught me how to warm myself by the lantern, how to make sure that the fishing line was tied tight, how to predict the fish on the line, and how to enjoy the harvest of the fish from the lake.

The mysteries of the lake revealed themselves to us many times in our fishing excursions. We were fishing one weekend with a longtime friend of his when his friend lost his fishing pole. The next weekend, I ended up catching his fishing pole from 40 feet under. My grandfather was amazed that I found it after only losing it the week before. It was as if a miracle had happened right there in the boat.

My grandfather always had a sacred place for us to connect with nature. He is a great representation of who I am to the elements. With him, I have created a vehicle for the understanding of the depth of my relationship to the air, *the water, the fire, the earth, gravity, time, and Spirit*. Relating to the seven elements allows access to building relationship with the plants, the animals, and to all the beings outside of humanity, even the star nations. There is great peace in understanding who we are in our reflection in the elements.

In the grand scope of things, if we really believed that we were all one, and if we practiced the truth of oneness without having to dissolve our personal identity or force others to dissolve there tribal or cultural identity, the Earth and all life would have few problems to solve. We would live in peace. Since my spiritual awakening, I have known this truth, yet for years I battled with the people who were called to love me the most. I warred against seeing myself in them; the discounting of their experience kept me submerged in the violence of separation. I fed upon the victimhood of my life until I could no longer breathe within the dense air of self-conflict that engulfed me. It wasn't until I realized that by battling within my *Sacred 7*, I was only battling myself. Now, with years of understanding the practice, I am at home with the design of my life. I am closer to who I really am and further from the violence, drugs, and alcohol that once clouded my system and forced me to stop far short of my human potential. Within all of us, there is so much more room to grow with than what we experience on the surface.

***

Now, that you have a preliminary understanding of *The Sacred 7* and how I have used it to transform my life, it is your turn. It is time to build *The Seven Sacred Containers of Self-Identity* for yourself in a way that serves, accelerates your spiritual journey and elevates the expression of who you are within yourself and in relationship to all around you.

CHAPTER 6

CREATING YOUR OWN SACRED 7

The Seven Sacred Containers of Self-Identity call empowers us to embrace members of our family lineage, understand them more deeply, and delve deeply into the spiritually abundant archetype of our relationship to them. A few years ago, during one of my visits to the *Havasupai Nation* in the Grand Canyon, an elder started up a conversation with me. He turned his ancient eyes to me and said, *I do not trust the spirits. Not all spirits or guides have your best interest in mind, and many will lead you astray. The people you should trust are your family and the Way.*

Intuitively, I felt that he was speaking of the family that is always with us. In that moment in the bottom of the Grand Canyon, I realized a spiritual truth that would change my life. I realized how logical it was to recognize that our greatest spiritual guides can be within our own family. Yet, for many of us, myself included, understanding the guidance of my *Sacred 7* meant having the courage to do some deep spiritual and energetic self-work. Facing our relationships within our families can be complicated and painful. Still, if we have the courage, it allows us to find a portal to our deepest power and peace.

As you proceed with *The Sacred 7*, you will find within yourself two profound guides that will help you in the process of confronting, healing, and elevating these relationships. These two can help you shift in a moment what would take most people years of consoling and therapy to overcome. These two precious companions are compassion and empathy; they are your alchemical tools to help you transform what would otherwise seem impossible to transform.

Compassion has given me the ability to overcome my feelings of remorse, guilt, shame, anger, and vengeance. It has helped me take what I considered negative and simply observe the energy that's associated with what I was experiencing. By opening myself to compassion, I have been able to utilize the energy of my feelings to heal my relationships with even those who have contributed trauma and abuse to my life.

Empathy can be a catalyst that connects us with the vibration of the Infinite. It helps us unsheathe ourselves from our addiction to victimhood. Many people hardly ever experience empathy and so their empathic response is underdeveloped in their minds and hearts. As we call empathy forward in our practice of *The Sacred 7*, we build the ability to displace the victim energy that captivates our consciousness and holds us prisoner to our own traumas. Like a true martial artist responding with fluid movement, the antagonist is transformed with gentle grace, the energy is harnessed, transmuted, and transformed to serve a great purpose. We look deep into the energy to find the place in which no harm is done. We use empathy to embrace and harness the energy of the trauma within us, and by doing so, harness the truth of our potential.

A martial artist is weakened if he judges the attack as negative—or even labels it as an 'attack' for that matter. Empathy gives you a level of freedom of judgment by helping you break the chains of your human conditioning that compels you to look at your experiences as either good or bad, negative or positive, dark or light. Empathy will allow you to step into the life of your ancestor—the one who chose to be one of your *Sacred 7* and chose to give you life— so you can be closer to who you are truly are.

For example, I believe that before my mother was born, she decided to take on an identity of being a drug addict. It was part of a spiritual agreement she made in the *Pre-Existence*—one she agreed to for my benefit. Why do I say that? Because there is a deep teaching inside of the container of my relationship to her. While I have countless memories of my mom's black and blue face from beatings from some boyfriend, the police, or another drug addict. How many times more times did that happen that I didn't even know about? How many times was she abused or raped that I never knew about? Loving me as a parent, she kept those incidents hidden from me so that I wouldn't have to suffer further. With compassion and empathy, I have gained the ability to see who she really was. I have been able to see more within her, feel more about her, and by doing so, receive more medicine from her. Compassion and empathy have allowed me to do that, and by doing so, heal myself.

The same is true with my father. With empathy and compassion, I have come to see that he struggled dearly in his life so that I could find my own medicine for myself. His life as a drug addict was full of suffering. Who knows how many times he was assaulted and how much trauma he went through in his life? Compassion has allowed me to hold him in a different light and gain a greater understanding of myself at the same time.

Always remember that this is your process—no one else's. The way you view your relationships can easily be completely different from your brother's or your sister's perspective. The depth with which you design your *Sacred 7* is about how deeply you are willing to go inside yourself to anchor into your reality a new design for all of your relationships in life.

***

Now is the time for you to create your own introduction and begin your own unique *Sacred 7* process. To begin the process, you will create an entry point for each one of the directions and containers of self. To do this, you'll create a symbol to use as your point of energetic connection that will act as a doorway into the world of spiritual connection and the design of who you are becoming. It will help you dive deeply into the energy and freedom that each container offers you. You will use your symbols in your meditations and even journaling to focus on, travel through, and hold space for transformation. Your symbols will also serve as building blocks for a crest and lineage you can pass to the next seven generations within your family.

We use very simple symbols—a few lines, drawn shapes,

or even dots on paper, drawn with intention, are enough. Symbols carry power. Here in my home in Arizona, the mountains are blanketed with thousands of symbols drawn by ancient hands. Many of them are very simple designs, but when you sit with them, your mind can travel to deep dimensions.

Then, you will focus your attention on calling in the energies of the directions, one at a time, building a metaphysical architecture with these energetic building blocks and constructing a new design for your life. By doing so, you take responsibility for building that which is you. I provide you with some ideas for articulating your vision for what each of the containers hold, but ultimately, what you want to fill your container of self with is up to you. You'll thoughtfully consider each container, read through journal entries (which I'll describe soon) and reflect on what has been revealed to you about each one of them. You can journal or even video what you feel is important to each of your containers, and you might want to share what power you see in yourself from that direction. It is literally all about you and your intentional design.

As you journey through *The Seven Sacred Containers* and *The Seven Sacred Directions*, you begin to create a holder of a perfect perspective of who you are. I invite you now to open the space for each container and let them come through you to share their wisdom.

***

We begin with the first three of the sacred containers, the spiritual ones: *Divine Feminine, Divine Masculine,* and *Sacred Child*. These first three resonate with the spiritual because of their deep mysterious nature. They are the great *I AM*, the mystery *Source* of all life, and that which made the design that is you. They are also the foundation from which you will view the other four directions. Their wisdom will allow you to be guided through the entire seven vantage points of *The Sacred Containers of Self-Identity*.

THE DIVINE FEMININE CONTAINER

As you journey into the place of the *Divine Feminine*, the *Below* space, you find that you are the very same force that created all of life. Within the *Divine Feminine*, you have come into an agreement with all that is nurturing in the universe. It is a place of power and it is the beginning of the journey to *manifest your medicine*. The truth of your suffering will become clear to you because, as you have experienced love and joy, you have also awakened to the tragedy of the human experience and the illusion and confusion of this reality. Now, you can begin to dissolve that illusion and experience the sovereignty of understanding that you are the mother of your own destiny.

The Divine Feminine is represented in your relationship to the one who gave birth to you: your mother. The *universe* was once a void darkness without consciousness. Then it put a circle around itself and said *I AM*. From there, it produced all the forms of sacred geometry until, in its replication process, it created you. *Why?* Simply and complexly because it wanted to love and be loved. The reason that we can find beauty in the darkness is because we were birthed from the darkness of the womb. So, it is time to forgive yourself for the conflicting thoughts of what your mother did or did not do for you. It is time to stop thinking about the feminine human being who gave birth to you. It is time to begin feeling that the love of the *Universe* is manifested through the *Divine Mother* who gave life to you and give yourself permission to feel the *Divine Feminine* within yourself.

By creating the *Divine Feminine* presence within yourself, you enhance your relationship with your actual mother. You give yourself the perspective tool of learning from her point view of you. During this process, the hurt of neglect may try to interfere and captivate you. You may find yourself deep in internal battle of recognizing her for who she really is or was. You may need to balance that pain with the compassion and the deep empathy of looking at yourself from her eyes, that is, from the *Sacred Below*, to give you that wisdom. See yourself as her, overwhelmed and unable to give. Feel the pain that was the cause of her being the person she is, and you will begin to free yourself from the confines of the victimhood and be catapulted to the brightness and beauty of self-mastery.

If you have, or had, a challenging relationship with your mother, it manifests in the obstacles in your soul's path— only to help you find the nurturing side of yourself. If you had a critical mom, you can see from the perspective of the *Divine Feminine* all the qualities that gave your mom that "critical" distinction in your mind. That vantage point allows you to reframe your *Divine Feminine* aspect into the one you turn to when you need gentle encouragement, a nurturing mother, or a mother full of wisdom.

The sweat lodge ceremony mimics the experience of going into the *Below* place. It is a place of purification and represents being inside the mother's womb. I often think about my mother when I am in the sweat lodge; I think about the suffering that she experienced in her life, the roads that she chose to take, all of which would seem so meaningless if I did not find my medicine.

Now, I am so grateful to be able to see myself from the perspective of the *Divine Feminine*. As a man, the mysteries of the feminine are close yet distant. They are close in that we, too, are feminine in design, but they are distant in our ability to understand the vastness of the womb, the cycles, and the mysteries of the feminine. Only through understanding the perspective of this *Sacred Direction* can we begin to truly understand the sacrifice and courage of our mothers.

For those who have had the pain of addiction, abuse, absent parents, rape or incest, know that you, too, can design a representation of mother to serve you. By doing so you, can break the cords to your inner victim and find your medicine in the relationship. Learn from her. She was brought to you as teacher, and as you let *Spirit* guide you through your process, the steps you need to take to manifest a feminine guide for yourself will become clear. Within all of the challenges that your soul has manifested in the design of your mother, there is an ultimate perfection that is beyond our human understanding. And it takes a lifetime of understanding to manifest the rich layers of self-revelation that this process will bring inside the container of the *Divine Feminine*.

Not having a connection to your *Divine Feminine* can create an imbalance in the protective or masculine side of yourself. You might be reactively overprotective so much that you don't do the things that you want to do. Maybe you stop yourself from experiencing life. This is the masculine living outside of the balance that is available inside the trinity of *The Seven Sacred Containers*. Lack of the *Divine Feminine* connection can also be reflected in a tendency to not take care of yourself. Coming back into alignment with the nurturing aspect of yourself reconnects you with the soft voice of your inner *Divine Feminine* so you are free to engage in life's adventures.

Create your symbol

On a blank piece of paper, draw a symbol to represent a portal through which the *Divine Feminine* aspect of yourself can express itself. This symbol will act as a window into the dimension of the *Divine Feminine* and a doorway into viewing yourself with the nurturing qualities that your soul wants for you. It will be a portal to find your medicine and purpose in ceremony, which I'll describe a little later. Use the direction of the *Below* place to guide you. Put your hands upon the earth, feel into the ground, and use your breath to become one with the direction. Call upon your mother to help you find your symbol. Ask her to guide you in the process and help you understand what to draw, how to move your hand, to help you find the portal to connect to yourself.

If you did not know your mother, or if you don't know her name, you'll need to create a name to use in your introduction. To do so, find a safe a place to sit quietly and meditate on the qualities of your *Divine Feminine* aspect. Bring an image to mind that you'll use as the energetic portal for your designated mother. You might see a unicorn, a dolphin, a color, or something completely different. Don't let judgment stop you. Write the name of the image somewhere on your piece of paper. This will be the name you will use when you learn to introduce yourself.

Questions to meditate on

Spend some time in meditation on the Divine Feminine aspect of your *Sacred 7*. Use these questions as a launching point of inquiry and then journal your answers.

- *What do I feel from the Below space? What feelings come up for me?*
- *What has my mom taught me about the Divine Feminine that serves my process?*
- *What can I do to embrace the Divine Feminine?*
- *How can I nurture myself or others? What does the Divine Feminine within me look like?*
- *What actions can I take today to demonstrate self-nurturing love?*
- *What is a practice I can incorporate into my life to remind myself of being more nurturing?*

THE DIVINE MASCULINE CONTAINER

The Divine Masculine is found in the *Above* place, the place of *Father Sky*, the infinite sower of the seeds of life. Through this container, we look at ourselves and see the infinite possibility of solutions to the challenges of life. Your *Divine Masculine* aspect is the protector, the decision-maker, and the holder of the logical mind. It is in every one of us, regardless of physical gender. From the vastness of the Above space, you awaken it within you and become champion of the battle fields of self-protection. You are the embodiment of masculinity formed by the fires of life. *The Divine Masculine* was the light that first broke through the womb, the power of the action of creation, protection and embodying strength, and the logical mind.

This part of you is the observer of your triggers and the voice that predicts the outcomes of your feelings. It is the one that stops the impulses and the one that takes action. As you come into alignment with the *Divine Masculine* representation within *The Seven Sacred Containers*, you let go of the voice of judgment and discover the voice of reason. You let go of the teachings of those outside of yourself and find meaning and purpose within yourself.

When you access your *Divine Masculine*, you help to restore the fullness of your incarnation in the human experience. You turn away from the perspective of the victim and leave abandonment behind you.

Create your symbol

On a blank piece of paper, draw a symbol to represent a portal through which the *Divine Masculine* aspect of yourself can express itself. This symbol will act as a window into the dimensional energies of the *Divine Masculine* and be a doorway into viewing yourself with the logical qualities that your soul wants for you. It will be a portal to find your medicine and purpose in ceremony. Use the direction of the *Above* place to guide you in this practice. Reaching to the sky, looking above, breathing in the expanse of the *Above* place, feel into the stars and the sun and call upon your connection to your father to help you in the process of finding your symbol.

Meditative practice

Sit and meditate on your relationship to the *Divine Masculine* and to your father. Ask what you have learned and how you might apply these teachings to serve yourself and others. Ask yourself what you can do to father yourself and how you can practice it today. Ask yourself if you are feeling protected. Ask what about your life would help you feel safer. Ask if it is logical that you feel unsafe. If you know it isn't logical, then ask yourself if it's okay to practice the steps of whatever it is you need to do to feel safe. You are your protector. You are your own *Divine Masculine* and now you must find that energy. Journal your answers.

If you did not know your father, or if you didn't have someone you considered a father figure, you'll need to create a name to use in your introduction. To do so, find a safe a place to sit quietly and meditate on the qualities of your *Divine Masculine* self-aspect. Bring an image to mind that you'll use as the energetic portal for your designated father. You might see a celestial being, an angel of some sort or, a dolphin, a color, or something completely different. Don't let judgment stop you. Write the name of the image somewhere on your piece of paper. This will be the name you will use when you learn to introduce yourself.

THE DIVINE CHILD CONTAINER

The child is represented in the *Inside* place, that place within your heart that is completely intimate and vulnerable. In its innocence, this part of you has the ability to survive, grow, and thrive.

Within *The Seven Sacred Containers, the Sacred Child* holds the playful spirit and simply believes in the *Divine*. So close to the *Source* within the *Trinity*, you are the foundation of feminine and masculine because, without your child self, creation has no container to manifest. Together in their fullness, the *Divine Feminine* and *Divine Masculine* unify to create a perfect presentation of the power of the *universe*.

You are the embodiment of the creative forces of life.

The *Inside* place holds the space for that which is pure. It is the *divine power of the child* in submission to the will of the *universe*. You are laughter that brings changes and the voice that cries. You are tantrums that are safe to be and you are joy that is safe to be without reason. You are *infinite possibility* and the blank page in which your masterful hand will create the story of a thousand lifetimes.

Create your symbol

On a blank piece of paper, draw a symbol to represent a portal through which the *Divine Child* aspect of yourself can express itself. This symbol will act as a window into the dimensional energies of the *Divine Child* and as a doorway into viewing yourself with the playful qualities that your soul wants for you. It will be a portal to find your medicine and purpose in ceremony. Use the direction of the Above place to guide you in this practice. Holding your hands on your heart and embracing the child within you, breathing in the expanse of the Inside place, feel your cells, your organs, and your bones. Go deep into feeling your own body. Feel at home here. Call upon your connection to your child that felt able to play and be free and imagine a better, more abundant life. Call upon your *inner child* to help you in the process of finding your symbol.

If you did not know the meaning of your name you can research it. It might be extremely revelatory for you to understand the definition of your name and how it applies to your life. My name is *Andrew*, which means *strong man*. My last name, *Ecker*, a German name, and it means *the corner*. I have learned that the walls of the corner are my heritage. One wall is *Native American* while the other is *European American*. This gives me a comfortable place in the middle. If, after you've researched your name, you don't want to use this name in your introduction, you may rename yourself. To do so, you must sit in quiet place and search for the parts of you that serve your greatest good. Search until you find the perfect name. This won't be hard but it might take time. You are a complex human being and in that complexity you must find some meaning and direction, which is what this practice is all about. *So be patient.*

Questions to meditate on

Here are a few questions to meditate on and inquire into about your *Divine Child*. Journal about the answers you get.

- *Is my inner child feeling both nurtured and protected?*
- *Can I play? Dance? Sing? Can I drum, pray, and feel comfortable?*
- *What can I do to practice play today?*
- *What can I do help my inner child believe again?*
- *Can I give myself and others the benefit of the doubt?*
- *Is there something I haven't done simply because I haven't felt safe enough or loved enough?*
- *Is there a place that I can take my inner child to play and be free?*

THE MOTHER'S MOTHER CONTAINER

As I've mentioned, the first three containers embody the *spiritual directions* and are the foundation for the remaining containers of The Sacred 7. Once we've engaged the spiritual directions, we find ourselves in the *East* again, where we experience ourselves anew. This is the first container that we work on to intentionally design ourselves for our relationships, other than our relationship to ourselves.

Your mother's mother guides you to fulfill the direction of the *East*. *She is the embodiment of who you are to new people.* This container is where you begin to form the formless energy of thought into the intentional energies that will be seen and felt outside of yourself. By declaring your *Sacred 7* intention to the world and speaking the name of your maternal grandmother, you give life to this purpose. All the energies of the *East* will hold this space for you from within your intentional design.

In my lineage, it would be said that our mother's mother is the one who we are born "from." Your mother's mother was the womb in which the womb that gave birth to you was born from. She is the closest clan member within the ancient design and her symbol will be the name of your first clan.

As we sculpt our lives out of the brokenness, shame, and defeat we have experienced, *we rise up to the clarity of new beginning in the East*. Trusting in the power of our will, and with the help of connection to *Source*, we design our reality to hold to the principle that people we meet are falling deeply in love with us the minute they see us. With the grace and skill of a master craftsman, we are called to challenge the *energetic architecture of reality* to include the choice of our consciousness to show the truth of what it means to be a new opportunity. The shyness that once gripped us in the imbalances of the *Divine Masculine* and *Divine Feminine* are now gone and we are free to play in the newness of friendship that fosters a lifetime of meaning.

Every thought that you bring to the place of the *East fortifies the beauty of your incarnation*. You are a new creation and whole and perfect in every way. The people who are new to you see you as having something for them to learn from. You have a natural magnetic quality that brings into your field people who are of greatest help to build your optimal life.

Your maternal grandmother is the energetic identity that represents you to the new people in your life. Now, perhaps you have felt shy, insecure, or less than others. Or perhaps you have struggled to say something to a new person you find attractive. Choosing to create this portal inside your life will help to bring balance and reduce your tendency to miss chance encounters. In turn, it will stop the wheels of self-doubt from turning.

When we miss an opportunity to share with someone out of fear or self-judgment, it is usually because we have not set the foundation of the trinity. Fortifying your self-view, not from your own flawed perspective, but from the perspective of the newness of life expressed through the *East*, is profound. This access point gives you the ability to say to yourself that you are considering the possibility that people love seeing you as an opportunity. By doing so, you begin the process of not hearing the damaged voice that continues to turn the wheel of self-doubt, grinding at the grief of missed opportunity, but instead you begin the process of feeling the love of new relationships. When you are around and you are enjoyable to be with, people are attracted to the gentleness of the *East*.

This practice might be a challenge for those who have spent years masking themselves in self-doubt. That in turn may have led to self-medicating with drugs, alcohol, money, shopping, new friends, or even having sex with

CREATING YOUR OWN SACRED 7

people as a way of masking the need for intimacy. If you have wandered for years looking for relationships that are meaningful but only connect with shallow people, it is most likely because you are not practicing intimate conversation yourself. It becomes very important to listen carefully from the perspective of what you are to other people. Think about your own programming. Are you seeing new friends or new enemies? Are you projecting that people are mean, cruel, angry, or dangerous? If so, does it still serve you?

I have been abused many times, yet I have learned that seeing new people as abusers only leads to more abuse. The soul becomes attracted to the frequencies that it produces. *The East grandmother* has held a space of reckoning of these energies within myself. She has allowed me to see myself through her gentle eyes of newness as *she rests in the East and governs the gentle new friends and family that emerge in my life.*

If you will work with this *Eastern grandmother* to fortify this space, the storms of life will come, but the skills of navigating them will be available for the rest of your human journey. Finding the compass will be as simple as just listening to her voice. Remember, this is a practice. *Be gentle with yourself and continue to love the newness of your new-found perspective.*

When you see a person you don't know, you might have feelings that come up such as racism, fear, hatred, or disconnect. You know these feelings and thoughts are no good for you, yet you do not know what to do. I am excited to tell you that by becoming a whole person again, many of these struggles will fade away. So, practice the design, sit with this idea of matriarchal grandmother representing a *metaphysical architecture.* She is the holder of wisdom for your life. Maybe you have never met her, or maybe she has been cruel or unable to be supportive. These judgments and feelings are ultimately teachings that will become the truth of your medicine for your human brothers and sisters. The tools that you learn from her will be revealed in time. But first you must design in your mind a process that is going to serve you.

Create your symbol

On a blank piece of paper, draw a symbol to represent a portal through which the energies of *East* will come through. This is the symbol of the new person that people will meet in your life and aspects of the person you want to design yourself to be will gather in this symbol. You can create any type of symbol, drawing, or shape that you'll use to allow the energetic spirit body to ground into becoming your reality, giving her a place to call home. As you energetically define your symbol, you create a depth that allows her energy to flow through it. She is eternal within the space that is beyond time and her medicine needs to be shared with your human family.

This symbol will act as a window into the dimensional energies of the East, the place in which your mother's mother holds space for you. It will be a doorway into viewing yourself with the energetic qualities of newness, and it will be a gateway into the *metaphysical architecture* of how you are going to be in perfect relationship with beings who newly interact with you. You won't need to guess anymore about what people think of you because you will know that they see the qualities of your own design. Use the direction of the *East* to guide you in this practice.

Writing exercise

So now it's time to get to work designing your matriarchal grandmother, the vehicle and container for the energetic body of who you are to new people. Sit down and list the attributes of your grandma that you love and all that she has given to you. Then write all that you truly hate: the parts of her that you cannot stand. If she made you eat green beans, write it down. If you did not know her, write that down along with all that you missed because she was not there. Then write out the parts of her that you want to design for yourself now. The most important thing is that you hold the space for yourself inside of this relationship. In other words, she is a reflection of a guide into your life not vice versa. She is the representation of who your highest self wants to create for new people that you want to see, feel, and know.

Meditative practice

Once you have your list, spend some time sitting with this being and reflecting upon the portal symbol or totem for your new energetic body.

Holding your hands to the *East*, breathing in the expanse of what you see in the dawning of the sun, pull in the newness of who you are. Feel your perfect relational self to all that is new. Feel into your cells, your organs, and your bones. Go deep into the feeling of your own body. Feel at home here. Call upon your connection to your matriarchal grandmother to give you permission to be a new reborn. Made by perfect intention, you are molding a great sculpture of yourself in the *East*. Ask for the symbol and draw it on a piece of paper to signify your *new self*.

If you did not know her name you will need to find a name for her in a good way. You can do so by inviting her to come to you through meditation. So, after you have drawn your symbol and created the energy of this new reflection of self, sit quietly in a safe place and ask her to show you her name. She may show herself to you in a vision with your eyes closed, or she might be the first thing you see when you open your eyes. Either way, you can attach the word "grandma" to this vision and in doing so you will have a name to speak in your introduction.

Your maternal grandmother is the keeper of *East*. She is waiting to share her *divine medicine* with you. I invite you to open the space for her and let her come through to share her wisdom. *It is time to redesign in depth and clarity that which will assist you in your life path.*

Questions to meditate on

Take some time to meditate on these questions about your experiences with new relationships:

- *Who am I to the new people I meet?*
- *How can I show myself as transparent and real to those new in my path?*
- *Am I energetically available for new relationships?*
- *Can I see Creator God in the new people on my path?*
- *Is the Creator showing me the beauty in new people?*
- *Am I curious about new people?*

THE FATHER'S MOTHER CONTAINER

Your fathers' mother holds the sacred space for your family. She is the womb through which your father manifested, and she is the gatekeeper of the energies of the *South*—the place in which your close relations hold their medicine and wait for it to be realized in you. When you form the energetic manifestation of this part of yourself, you are defining the optimal self for you to be within your family. You are being your perfect self, full and complete, without insecurities and pain. You are free from those who have triggered you for years and their burdens. You are complete in the wholeness of who you are. Imagine the beauty of being your truest self to your family instead of being who they want or expect you to be.

Before the creation of the world, it was foretold that you would be a part of the woven story of your family. It was your decision before you incarnated into this form to be a part of that woven blanket and to share in its tragedies, victories, joy, and pain.

In the direction of the *South*, you become the daughter, son, niece, nephew, cousin, grandson, granddaughter. Your relationship to family is sculpted and guided by the hand of conscious intention and molded by the great source of divine love. You are asking the *universe* to fill your conscious mind with the greatest love possible for your family and cut the spiritual bindings that hold you stuck, such as neglect, trauma, and suffering. Now you are the victorious creation that you have always wanted to be for your family. Like a beacon of light, you stand in your fullness as a whole human being; strengthened in your sovereignty, you are able to live in meaningful relationship to those closest to you.

Many of us run from the medicine of the teachings of

our family. We think, *Why would I be born to these people?* Some even say that theirs is not their family at all. Our father's mother teaches us that we made the decision to manifest our family and that the pain and insecurities we've suffered are blessings to our lives. It can be a challenging perspective to take on, of course, when the abuse, hurt, trauma and pain of life engulfs us. It was for me. By letting go of the perspective of my victimhood and by seeing the empowered view of my grandmother in the *South*, I have found a new and fresh understanding of who I am that softens the blows of the past.

With the help of my father's mother of the *South*, I learned why I chose the medicine of my family. I learned why I chose to live the life I lived, why I chose to bear the burden of an abused child, why I was able to survive suicide, and why I was able to be bounced around as a child without a real home of my own. I learned why the burdens were my choice. This view of my *sacred self* through the eyes of my father's mother broke the chains of family shame and brought comfort to me once again.

It is time for you, too, to let go of your traumas and embrace a new perspective. She is waiting in the *South* with so much medicine but because you have not held space for her, she can only wait until you choose to do so. It is time to reconstruct her in a way that serves the greater process.

Your father's mother will bring you the wisdom you seek about interacting with your family. She will bring you clarity about feeling compassion for people, even your sexual, physical, and mental abusers. With the help of her insight and perspective, you can let your gentle self unfold into a new relationship with your family and end the karmic curse that has plagued you.

Create your symbol

On a blank piece of paper, draw a symbol to represent a portal through which the energy of who you are to your family will manifest. You will bring forth your father's mother through the design of this symbol. Let it be a portal for how you want her to be. This symbol will act as a window into the dimensional energies of your personal intention of who you are to your family and be a doorway into viewing yourself with the qualities and nature of what you have always wanted to be for your family. Before you know it, your mind will create that which you have honored. This is your process and your design. Use the direction of the *South* to guide you in this practice.

Meditative practice

Holding your hands to the *South* and embracing the vast energies of the *South*, begin breathing in the expanse of the of this place. Feel your cells, your organs, and your bones. Go deep into feeling your own body. Feel at home here. Imagine yourself in perfect relationship with your family. Let go of all that does not serve you and breathe into all that does. Your father's mother is here in the *South* to hold space for you and to help you live in relational beauty with all that you are to your family. *You are free now to imagine a better, more abundant life.* Call upon your father's mother here in the *South*. She will guide you and help you in the process of finding your symbol.

If you did not know the name of your father's mother, you will need to find a name for her in a good way. Do so by inviting her to come to you through meditation. As before, sit quietly in a safe place. With your symbol in front of you, ask her to show you her name. She might show you herself in a vision with your eyes closed or you might see her when you open your eyes. However, you receive it, attach the word "grandma" to this vision and you are ready to use it in your introduction.

Writing exercise

As you've done before, write out both the positive and negative attributes of your relationship with your father's mother. Write down what she means to you. You might also feel the pain of your abusive uncle, your hurtful father, the pain of grandfather in her design. Let out what she didn't do and what she did do. Then, when you are done, draw your symbol for her.

If you have never known her, write out the parts of her that you can design for yourself now. The most important thing is that you hold the space for yourself inside of this relationship. In other words, she is a reflection of a guide into your life, not vice versa. *She is the representation of who your highest self wants to create for new people that you want to see, feel, and know.*

Meditative practice

Take some time to meditate on these questions about your relationship to your family and journal your thoughts, insights, and feelings.

- *Who am I to my family?*
- *What can I share with my family that will draw us closer?*
- *How can I serve my family? How do they serve me?*
- *What medicine do I have to help my family live a good life?*
- *How can I love my family in deeper way?*

THE MOTHER'S FATHER CONTAINER

Through the direction of the *West*, the direction of your mother's father, you bring through the embodiment of who you are to community. You begin to define yourself in way that gives life to your dreams. You are free to share your heart, your mind, and your spirit generously and you are strong enough to allow the criticism and judgments to fall away. You can see into the energetic the perfect design of how you are to your community.

For some, this grandfather has been waiting within the spirit for years to activate his medicine. He has been on the outside of your life, patiently waiting to guide, comfort, and protect. For some, he has always been there and will continue to offer divine perspective and reasoning. For others, he offers a new perspective of self: the container of the community as the *guardian of the community*.

There are many reasons for not feeling safe in community and not feeling safe enough to open up to the community members. We search deeply for meaningful relationships and blame the people around us for being shallow. We look at our coworkers, those on our softball league, our church friends, business relationships, or people in our band or drum circle, and wonder why no one has opened up to us. We find out a friend was divorced, lost a parent or loved one, and we were not told. We wonder why—when we ourselves have withheld our authenticity from the community all along.

If you have not found a community for yourself, you can start one around this book. You can share this book and start a community. You can ask the grandfather of the *West* to guide and protect you and help you to create a community. But first you must do the work and give life to this *sacred container of self-identity*. The process is always about looking back at yourself from the direction at hand.

You chose this grandfather and you made a commitment to seeing yourself through the struggles of this incarnation. What has he taught you about yourself in this life? Was he abusive or caring or religious or secular? Did you know him? There is always a lesson in the patterns of the soul. There is always a place of restoration to take you back to the wholeness that is the essence of all of things. Maybe he was sexually abusive or hurt you in ways that never could be washed away. If so, you can allow your body to go within that place and find the compassion of understanding the sickness of what it takes to do that to a child, young adult, or teenager. You can realize that he was sick and in his sickness you have been given a chance to not hide the experience in guilt and shame, but to let the medicine of the experience become a guide to you in your life.

Let the medicine of the pain of your deepest trauma raise your vibration so you can help those in your community. We will never get over these wounds; they are too deep. But they can be transformed, since energy can never be destroyed it only changes. For the sake of humanity, I ask you to allow the trauma to change into medicine so we all may heal and overcome in this beautiful process of life.

The grandfather that holds the *West* shares with us the necessity of walking boldly into the community and sharing our medicine. In him, we build up a fortified architecture to share outside the comfort of the new relationships in the *East*, and the close ties to the family in the *South*. In his place, we join the friendships, community, and other people who have gathered due to some common goal or experience. He is the one who creates our tribe. He helps us mold the idea of the expanse of tribal experience.

As tribe, community, and human race, you can let the expanse of your mother's father view open your medicine. Let his teachings transcend this mundane physical experience and open you to the wisdom of this guardian grandfather in the *West*.

Create your symbol

On a blank piece of paper, draw a symbol to represent a portal through which the energies of the *West* will manifest. This is the gateway into the perfection of who you are to the community. This is how your job, your place of worship, your friends, and your tribe sees you. Your symbol represents your perfect relationship to community and how you see yourself from the perspective of the *West*. It will act as a window into the dimensional energies of the relationship you have with community.

Meditative practice

Use the direction of the *West* to guide you in this practice. Holding your hands on your heart and embracing all the qualities of the relationships you have developed and are now intentionally creating in community, breathe into the expanse of the *West*. Feel your cells, your organs, and your bones. Go deep into feeling your own body. Feel at home here. Call upon your connection to your mother's father. He will guide you into this place.

Now go deep within your third eye to see the *metaphysical architecture* of your divinely-inspired symbol of your connection to the *West*. Take some time to draw out that symbol. Your challenge is to see this symbol within yourself and bring it through to this physical reality. Looking at this symbol, you must see into the feelings that come up. You are fortifying this landing space for the reflection of yourself—molding and creating who you are in relationship to the community. If feelings come up, remember that this is a process and if these feelings arise, then they are an offering of acceptance. Accept the feelings as a process within the cycle. *Give yourself permission to sit with your feelings and know that the lessons are about finding your medicine.*

Writing exercise

If you have never known your mother's father, write out the reflection in yourself that you would most like to see. The most important thing is that you hold the space for yourself inside of this relationship. In other words, *he is the representation of who your highest self wants to be in relationship with community.*

If you don't know his name, you will need to find a name for him. As before, invite him to come to you through meditation. First draw your symbol and create the energy of this new reflection of yourself. Then sit quietly and ask him to show you his name. When you have it, you'll attach the word "grandfather" to this image, and you'll have a name to mention in your introduction.

Meditative practice

In the *West*, we inquire into these questions. Journal about the answers you get.

- *Who am I to community?*
- *How do I show up for that I don't need to love but I can decide to?*
- *What can I do to build my community?*
- *How can I show my true heart to those that are in my community?*

CREATING YOUR OWN SACRED 7

- *What medicine do I have to share with my community?*
- *Where can I see Community?*

THE FATHER'S FATHER CONTAINER

You have made it through six of *The Seven Sacred Containers*. By the time you get here to the seventh, you are in a place of deep feeling and vibrant human living. In order for this container to be fully realized, learning to love and live to the fullness of the other six containers is a must.

In this container, we look at ourselves from the perspective of the grandfather of the *North*, the father's father. This is the *Sacred Container* that *holds your identity and relationship to the elements* and everything that is created through them. This grandfather waits for you to open up this medicine and see yourself through the vastness of the elements: *the earth, air, water, and fire.* These four basic elements create the tangible world; they are the fundamental building blocks of the trees, the winds, the rolling waves of the oceans, and our animal friends. It is through the grandfather of the *North* that we can see ourselves through their eyes and the eyes of the ocean, the moon, and the fire burning in the sky.

Our father's father helps us understand who we are to the elements: to *air, water, fire, and earth.* In this direction, we explore a deeper relationship with life through the elements. We learn to speak to the elements, and most importantly, to listen to them. We dive deep to reflect upon the *grand space of consciousness* that reveals not just what it means to be human, but what it means to be an earthling and a *citizen of the infinite universe.* We go beyond just feeling the emotions of our human relatives to understanding the feeling of the entire *universe*.

This expansive perspective opens us to the awesome vastness of creation itself and to seeing that vastness within our experience of being human. As we work within *The Seven Sacred Containers*, our thoughts begin to materialize and manifest right before our eyes. The beauty of this manifestation is held in the basic elements and in our understanding of our relationship to them.

With your willingness to connect on a deep level, the deep mysteries of the elements are revealed to you along with an amazing, limitless pool of revelatory experience. Feel the wind and know that it is carrying a message to you. Listen to the fire and dance to the songs of the flames. Make offerings to the earth and see the birds, the animals, and the insects as people in a great story of your life. See yourself in the beauty of the hummingbird, in the sacredness of the eagle, in the picture on the wall. *Feel your profound connection to all that is and be embraced, informed, and uplifted by it.*

Create your symbol

On a blank piece of paper, draw a symbol to represent a portal through which the energies of the *North* will manifest. This symbol will become a window into the dimensional energies of your relationship to the elements and a doorway for you to view yourself with the powerful qualities of living in perfect relationship with the elements. These are qualities that your soul wants for you. Use the direction of the *North* to guide you in this practice.

Meditative practice

Holding your hands to the *North*, breathing in the expanse of the space of your relationship to the animals, the planet, the air, the water, the fire, the earth, gravity, time, and spirit. Imagine you're the perfect representations of yourself and see yourself vibrating intentionally with the earth and star nations. Design this for yourself and begin to live in complete relationship with all your relations outside the human experience. Feel your cells, your organs, and your bones. Go deep into feeling your own body. Feel at home here. Call upon your connection to your father's father. Be free to imagine a better, more abundant life.

Sit with the practice. Slow down and ask your body to give the process over to you and give yourself obediently to this work. You have the courage and the ability. *The grandfather of North holds certain codes for your identity* that are only understood when the other six directions and perspectives of self are designed. This work in the *North* is grand and I pray for you to fully realize the potential for all human beings and the planet herself.

Writing exercise

If you have never known your father's father, write out your ideal representation of your relationship to the elements. Remember, the most important thing is that you hold the space for yourself inside of this relationship. He is the representation of who your highest self wants to create for your relationship to the elements.

If you don't know his name, invite him to come to you through meditation. Draw your symbol and create the energy of this new reflection of yourself. Then sit quietly and ask him to show you his name. When you have it, you'll attach the word "grandfather" to this image, and you'll have a name to mention in your introduction.

Questions to meditate on

Meditate on these questions having to do with the *North* direction:

- *Do the elements know my name?*
- *Am I in relationship with the water, the air, the fire, and earth?*
- *What can I do to foster a deeper relationship with the planet and everything that I relate to—seen and unseen?*

As we are made in the image of *God*, we hold the beauty that allows us to resonate with the frequencies of the very basic elements of this world. They are like us in their true essence. Within the expanse of your mind, you can find these represented within yourself.

As we journey through *The Seven Sacred Containers*, we realize we cannot see ourselves truly until we have the vastness of perspective that the *North* provides. Allow this perspective to engage you in this *Sacred Journey of Life* and to enhance what you are calling yourself.

PRACTICING YOUR INTRODUCTION IN CEREMONY

You've now been given all the tools you need to build your spiritual containers of self-identity. You are now ready to step out of the spiritual and energetic and into the vastness of reality of real life. To expand your practice, I invite you to practice your introduction in ceremony. Here's some guidance about doing that:

Begin by setting an intention for your ceremony to help free you from the captivity of this world and to allow you to enter into the limitless world of spirituality and energetic manifestation.

I like to begin all my ceremonial practices with a prayer and then light a smudge stick or some incense, and I recommend that you do, too. You might want to come up with your own words for your prayer. If it helps, here's what I say:

> *Thank you, Creator, for allowing me to enter into this prayer place that was founded before the creation of the world. Thank you, for allowing me to be in relationship with you. I thank you for the Gaan, the Kachinas, and the Yibechia, the holy angels of the land I stand upon. I thank you for the air, water, fire, and earth; for my mom, my dad, my grandmas, and my grandpas. I thank you for the Above place, the Below place, the Inside place, the East, the South, the West, and the North. Thank you for being a light to my footstep and a shield to protect me from the arrows that fly by night. Thank you for opening and closing doors for me. Beauty above, beauty below, beauty beside, beauty in front, beauty behind, beauty within. Thank you Mother Father God. Amen.*

Now, light your smudge or incense and begin your ceremony.

Standing towards the *East*, begin with the three spiritual containers, introducing yourself in the order of *The Sacred 7*. Make an effort to motion to or touch the place that you are introducing yourself to. For example, you'll say your mom's name, touch the ground, and say *the Divine Feminine*. Say your father's name, reach to the sky, and say *the Divine Masculine*. Say your own name, touch your heart, and say, *the Inside place*.

Still facing the *East*, continue with the remaining four directions. Say your maternal grandma's name and say, *I welcome the new people into my life that serve my optimal life. I invite new love and new prosperity.*

Face the *South* and say the name of your paternal grandmother. Ask her to guide you in your relationships with your family. Invite the family to be their greatest selves and invite yourself to be your greatest self. Ask for the help you need.

Face the *West* and call to your mother's father. Ask for the highest friends, community, and caring tribe to manifest. Ask your grandfather to guide you here. Invite your community, too. Ask for help in areas you need help with, such as your job, your school, your relationships.

Face the *North* and speak the name of your father's father. Ask to be in relationship with the elements: *the air, water, the fire, and the earth* and ask the animals and star people to help you, too. All the ones that crawl on the earth, swim in the sea, fly in the air, ask for your grandfather's guidance.

Close the ceremony with gratitude for all the parts of yourself working in harmony to help you live a better life.

Always begin your ceremony with your introduction and end with your introduction.

DESIGNING YOUR SYMBOLS

As you design each of the seven symbols for each one of the directions to use in ceremony, you will want to be intentional. Each symbol needs to be drawn inside a circle and each one given a name and a placement. Take your time, be patient, and the symbols will come to you at the right time. During the period of time you are birthing the symbols, keep a piece of paper with you at all times. Ask for the symbols and they will appear like guides upon the trail of life. Once you have your symbols, sit in front of them and meditate. Let them give you the energetic downloads as portals into the mysteries of life. Ask the *universe* to guide you through the symbols into a deeper relationship with yourself. Maybe for the first time in thousands of years, your family will have a new crest or totem to represent them that will speak to the next seven generations.

PRACTICING YOUR INTRODUCTION

On a night when you can see the moon and stars clearly, stand in an open field or somewhere that you can see an uninterrupted sky. Look upwards and take a look at the expanse of the universe and the beauty of the sky. Focus your thoughts and your eyes in a way that allows you to see as much of the sky as possible. Then practice your introduction. Introduce yourself to the moon, the stars, the star nations, and the heavenly host. In this sacred place, *proclaim your identity to the grandness of the universe.*

Now, sit in a comfortable place or lay on your back and meditate with the heavenly host. *Listen to the voice of your spirit.* Ask the stars for their names. Focus on one star, or the moon, and go deep into a place of relationship. Try to connect to the stars by creating a dialog in your mind that serves your relationship. Think of the beauty of the stars and your connection to the star nations. When you feel complete, journal what you find from this place.

CEREMONY FOR THE ELEMENTS

We have lost our connection to and harmony with the elements. Now it is time to regain that place of relational living. This next ceremony is more of description rather than a prescription. You can use it as a spiritual gateway into learning to relate to all the elements. While it's important to give each element personal attention, it's also valuable to address the elements together as equal parts to the beautiful story creation, and that's what I do in this way.

To start, set up your altar. Take a bowl, cup, or glass and put some water into it. This will be your water totem. Then light a candle to create the connection to the fire. Next find a symbol for the air, such as a chime or a feather. Next, you need a symbol for the Earth. I usually use an animal totem or a stone of some kind. Next, the three spiritual elements: gravity, time, and *Spirit*. For gravity, I use a scale or a measuring device. For time, I use an hour glass or watch. For *Spirit*, you can use whatever you feel comfortable with.

As you create your altar, be intentional with the placement of your items. Once it is done, step back and introduce yourself to each of the elements. I would encourage you to do eight separate introductions. Introduce yourself to all seven of them and then introduce yourself to the whole of all the elements. After you've done your introductions, speak to the elements as friends. Let them know that you did your best to create a safe and pleasant place for them and that this meeting is very important to you. You want to learn to present your needs with an expression of thankfulness and prayer. If you feel called to ask for forgiveness, for not living up to your relationships or mis-using your relationship, say it in a way of thanks, as in, *Thank you, elements, for allowing me to be forgiven and allowing me to be in relationship with you. Thank you for all you have done for me, my family, my community, and the planet.*

I invite you to sit and meditate at your altar. Feel the human suffering caused by living outside of relationship with the elements and also feel the thousands of years of our global ancestral harmony. Feel yourself coming back home to living as an earthling. Now and forevermore, the elements know your name. You're no longer just a job. *You are a member of the Earth family.*

***

After practicing these ceremonies, your introduction will become more fluid and you'll begin to establish a foundation for enjoying life and a resource for when life gets uncertain or painful. From now on, you will be able to call upon your introduction to ground your mind, spirit, and body and find your center in the universe. Use your *Sacred 7* like a prayer to establish who you are and awaken your potential.

There are many other ways I have used *The Sacred 7*. I have introduced myself to mountains, canyons, oceans rivers, lakes, hot springs, the dawn, the sunset, to people, in ceremony. Whenever I have wanted to connect in a deeper way, I use this powerful tool. *The Sacred 7* has made a huge a difference in my life and I hope it will for you, too. I am in humble gratitude for my ancestors, the *Apache Nde* people, who stood and kept these teachings across hundreds of years.

Before sweat lodge, I will often introduce myself to the fire and the stone people that are heated in the fire. In the lodge, I will introduce myself to the air, the *water, the fire, the earth, gravity, time, Spirit,* and to all the human beings. When you introduce yourself like this in ceremony, you will find that the elders will begin to connect with you in new ways. For those of you who have practiced medicine ceremony, P*eyote* or maybe *Ayahuasca*, or if you have used other medicines but have never introduced yourself to the ceremony or the medicine itself before, you may want to. At your next ceremony, use your *Sacred 7* to bring the power of the seven directions and your ancestors into your life. You will notice a difference in your process.

CHAPTER 7

THE GREAT AWAKENING

It might be shocking to learn that all your work with your *Sacred 7* does not promise you relief from your suffering entirely. You will always have emotions and you will always have the ability to suffer—that is the life of a human being. This process will help you manage everything within your emotional spectrum in a way that serves you, your community, and planet. As you begin the work, get ready to wake up to the power that resonates within your Sacred 7 and what it means to feel completely available to others and completely open to the challenges of life.

It is my hope that in your exploration of *The Seven Sacred Containers* that your life will begin to flow like water and your medicine will be revealed to you. Be gentle with yourself and give yourself time to design a *Sacred 7* that works for you. Remember that this is a lifetime process; you will find that being patient is one of your best traveling companions. It is about self-mastery, which is a journey of a lifetime.

We live in great time of prophecy and many of the mysteries of life are being told in front of our eyes. The Hopi Prophecy, The Black Snake, The Eagle and Condor and the prophecies of the Rainbow all speak to these times. Some say these prophecies were thought up by crazed Indians and hippie environmentalist and have no merit in today's life. I have felt the power of these prophecies and know what the fortified field of energetic manifestation creates. The ancestors have danced prayed and drummed these prophecies into the world and we are all here now for a reason. These are the times in which we must choose how we are going to live and what we are going to leave for the next 7 generations. It is time to awaken the power of our collective ancestral experience to find the path of beauty. I ask all of you to come back to remembering the ways of the earth to take in consideration all your relations and to use the power of *The Sacred 7*. To come back to the Great Hoop, to the medicine wheel and to live in peace with each other and planet.

***

The Sacred 7 is a movement about remembering from our ancestors what it means to be an Earthling. I invite you to join the movement and become a Perfect Seven. You can follow us on Facebook and Instagram and connect with us on our website, www.thesacredseven.com. We are faced with times where we all need to be in discussion to help the next seven generations survive. By joining our movement, we are coming together to share with each other the necessary resources of transformation that will help us all find redemption.

Made in the USA
Middletown, DE
22 March 2025